D1766000

nordic family
kitchen

MIKKEL KARSTAD
PHOTOGRAPHY ANDERS SCHØNNEMANN

nordic family kitchen

SEASONAL HOME COOKING

PRESTEL

MUNICH · LONDON · NEW YORK

foreword

Food and mealtimes have always been a big part of my life and that of my family. My mother always took the time to cook and made an effort to buy good ingredients to make wonderful meals, so as a child I got to taste a lot of different foods and developed a curiosity for trying new things.

When I was 12 or 13 years old, I was given my own 'dinner day', where I had to figure out what to make for dinner and what to buy, and I would spend most of the afternoon preparing the meal, which my mother, her husband and I would eat together while talking about what I had made and what I could maybe do better for next time.

This interest in food got me into culinary science and now I have been working for 30 years with some of the things I love best – people and food.

In my own family – Camilla and our four children, Oscar, Alma, Konrad and Viggo – food, of course, has a special place through my work, but especially in our home life, where Camilla and I always do what we can to ensure our children see and taste a range of different foods. Our travels have often been planned on the basis that there was a strong and exciting food culture in the country we were to visit, and we often take the children with us to the woods or the beach to collect edible things from nature.

We grow our own vegetables and herbs on our farm in Copenhagen and, for a change, we raised some chickens so we could have fresh eggs every morning. In this way, we have tried to arouse our children's interest in food and make it completely natural for them to try new things, to recognize that you have to make an effort to cook and to know about the ingredients you use.

I know that sometimes they think I can be a little bit demanding when I say, 'Now we are going to the forest again' or 'Just taste this new thing', but I can see that a great love of food has been awakened in all of them and they actually enjoy cooking, especially when we do it together and then afterwards sit down and spend time eating and chatting.

This book is full of recipes that are good for breakfast, lunch and dinner, for busy days and for days when you have time to go out into nature, gather ingredients and cook over an open fire.

The most important thing is that you spend some time every day cooking, making an effort to prepare a nice meal, using good local ingredients and, above all, eating it with your family and the people you care about.

Enjoy!

Mikkel

in the
garden

Growing things yourself and using them in your everyday meals gives you great joy and satisfaction, and it provides an opportunity for children to learn that even if you live in the middle of a big city, you can be self-sufficient in many ways. In our small garden we grow herbs and vegetables, and enjoy spending time in this quiet oasis within a busy city.

elderflower lemonade

WITH HERBS

MAKES 2–2.5 LITRES
(4–5 PINTS) OF LEMONADE
(diluted)

15 freshly picked elderflower heads
3–4 sprigs mint
3 organic lemons
600 g (21 oz) sugar
2 litres (4 pints) water

Cut the flowers from the elderflower heads, wash them carefully and put them in a bowl with the mint.

Slice the lemons and put in a pan with the sugar and water. Heat the water and sugar mixture just to boiling point, then add the elderflowers and most of the mint. Turn off the heat and let cool, then leave to infuse for 12 hours on the kitchen counter.

Strain the lemonade to remove the large pieces of lemon and mint before serving with a little water, the remaining mint leaves and ice.

The lemonade is also good frozen into moulds as homemade ice lollies for the kids. For the adults, the lemonade can be added to white wine, or served as a mixer with gin or vodka.

Keeps in the fridge for 4–6 weeks.

herb pesto

MAKES 1 LARGE GLASS
(500 ML)

5 large handfuls mixed herbs
2 slices day-old bread
25 g (1 oz) freshly grated parmesan
300 ml (1¼ cups) olive oil
salt and freshly ground pepper

Rinse the herbs in cold water and dry thoroughly. Remove the stalks if necessary and put the herbs in a blender, together with the day-old bread, parmesan, olive oil, salt and freshly ground pepper, and blend into a thick pesto.

Pour into a bowl and serve with grilled garfish (see page 18) and baked potatoes (see page 22).

grilled baked potatoes

WITH HERBS, JUNKET AND PARMESAN

SERVES 4

4 large baking potatoes
salt and freshly ground pepper
200 ml (¾ cup) junket
50 ml (3 tbsp) olive oil
several sprigs and 2 handfuls of
mixed herbs *(rosemary, sage, marjoram)*
40 g (2 oz) freshly grated parmesan

Heat the oven to 180 °C (360 °F). Wash the potatoes and place in an ovenproof dish, sprinkle with a little salt and bake in the oven for 1 hour or until soft.

While the potatoes are baking, season the junket with 2 tbsp olive oil, salt and freshly ground pepper. Remove the potatoes from the oven and let them cool.

Cut the cooled potatoes roughly into wedges and place in a cooking grate with the sprigs of herbs. Drizzle with a little olive oil and sprinkle with sea salt. Close the grate and grill the potatoes over a hot grill so that they take on a nice colour and are slightly crispy.

Take the potatoes off the grill and place on a platter. Serve with the junket, fresh herbs and freshly grated parmesan. Finally, drizzle with a little olive oil. Serve while the potatoes are still warm so the topping melts.

herb-grilled garfish

SERVES 4

3–4 whole garfish *(depending on size)*

3 handfuls herbs *(sweet cicely, bronze fennel, tarragon)*

50 ml (3 tbsp) olive oil

sea salt

Clean and gut the garfish, rinsing thoroughly in cold water to wash away any blood. Dry with a paper towel and divide into 3–4 long pieces. Put the fish on a plate and sprinkle with rinsed herbs, olive oil and sea salt.

Cook the fish on a hot grill pan for 3–4 minutes on each side, so they are nicely grilled on the surface but still lovely and juicy in the middle.

Transfer from the grill onto a plate, sprinkle with a little extra salt, olive oil and fresh herbs, and serve straight away.

Enjoy with grilled baked potatoes (see page 18), herb pesto (see page 16) and good bread.

elderflower and rosemary pancakes

WITH BAKED RHUBARB AND LEMON VERBENA SUGAR

MAKES 15–20 PANCAKES

BAKED RHUBARB

4–6 rhubarb stalks *(depending on thickness and size)*

50 g (2 oz) sugar

juice of ½ organic lemon

1 freshly picked elderflower head

The rhubarb can be made the day before you need it

LEMON VERBENA SUGAR

2 handfuls vervain/lemon verbena

50 g (2 oz) sugar

PANCAKES

400 g (2½ cups) flour

2 tbsp baking powder

75 g (3 oz) sugar

3 eggs

400 ml (1½ cups) milk

25 g (1 oz) melted butter

5 freshly picked elderflower heads

2 sprigs rosemary

butter for frying *(optional)*

For the baked rhubarb, heat the oven to 100 °C (210 °F). Cut the leaves and roots off the rhubarb and rinse the stalks in cold water. Dry thoroughly and slice the rhubarb into lengths of 7–8 cm (3 in). Place in an oven-proof dish, sprinkle with the sugar, lemon juice and elderflowers, and bake in the oven for 12–15 minutes until the pieces are just tender but still retain their shape and firmness. Remove the rhubarb from the oven and leave for 1–2 hours to absorb the flavour of the elderflowers and lemon.

For the lemon verbena sugar, combine the sugar and lemon verbena in a food processor and pulse for 1–2 minutes until you have a uniformly green and fragrant sugar.

For the pancakes, sift the flour and baking powder into a bowl and stir in the sugar. Beat the eggs and milk together and add to the flour little by little, stirring carefully. The consistency should be thick. Add the melted butter while whisking vigorously. Finally stir the elderflowers and rosemary into the batter.

Mix the batter well so that the elderflowers are evenly distributed throughout. Spoon a blob of batter approx. 10–15 cm (4–6 in) in diameter into a frying pan, and fry over a medium heat until the pancake has a nicely browned surface, adding a little extra butter if necessary so that it doesn't stick. Repeat until all the batter has been used.

Serve the pancakes warm with a little baked rhubarb and sprinkled with lemon verbena sugar.

breakfast

baked cherries

WITH YOGHURT, TOASTED BUCKWHEAT AND HEMP SEEDS

SERVES 4

200 g (7 oz) cherries

35 ml (2 tbsp) acacia honey

3 sprigs mint

2 sprigs redwood sorrel

1 organic lemon

800 ml (3⅓ cups) Greek yoghurt

2 tbsp hemp seeds

2 tbsp whole buckwheat groats

Heat the oven to 100 °C (210 °F). Rinse the cherries and transfer them to an ovenproof dish. Drizzle with the acacia honey and sprinkle with the mint and sorrel leaves. Slice the lemon into quarters and squeeze a little juice over the cherries. Then add the lemon pieces to the dish.

Put the dish with the cherries in the oven and bake for 15 minutes until the cherries are just warm and have absorbed the flavour of the honey and herbs. Remove the cherries from the oven and leave in the dish to cool.

Meanwhile, in a dry pan, toast the hemp and buckwheat for 3–4 minutes on a low heat until they start to release their aroma and pop a little. Remove the seeds from the pan and leave to cool.

Spoon the yoghurt into 4 bowls, add the cherries and cooking juice, then sprinkle the toasted seeds on top.

The cherries can be baked in advance and refrigerated until needed. They will keep for 2–3 weeks in the fridge.

granola

WITH OLIVE OIL, HONEY, SEEDS, COCONUT FLAKES AND BLACKCURRANTS

SERVES 4

70 g (½ cup) pumpkin seeds

70 g (½ cup) sunflower seeds

70 g (½ cup) sesame seeds

90 g (1 cup) coarse rolled oats

40 g (½ cup) coconut flakes

70 ml (4 tbsp) honey

½ tsp sea salt

50 ml (3 tbsp) olive oil

50 g (2 oz) freeze-dried blackcurrants

Heat the oven to 150 °C (300 °F). Toast all the seeds, oats and coconut flakes on a baking sheet for 7–8 minutes until golden and starting to release their aroma. Stir them periodically with a spoon so that everything is evenly toasted.

Meanwhile, in a pan, warm the honey until it starts to bubble a little. Add the sea salt and olive oil, stirring well so it mixes thoroughly with the honey.

Remove the baking sheet from the oven and pour the warm honey/ olive oil mixture over the toasted seed mix, stirring everything well. Then return the tray to the oven and toast the seed mix for a further 5 minutes until golden brown and lightly caramelized.

Take the granola out of the oven and leave to cool. Chop the freeze-dried blackcurrants and stir into the granola. Transfer the granola to a bowl or glass and serve with yoghurt for breakfast.

The granola can easily be made in a larger quantity so you have enough to last a couple of weeks.

porridge with plums

BAKED WITH WILD ROSE PETALS AND HAZELNUTS

SERVES 4

BAKED PLUMS
10 fresh plums
10 wild rose petals
juice and zest of 1 organic lemon
50 g (2 oz) sugar

PORRIDGE
90 g (1 cup) flaked oats
90 g (1 cup) flaked spelt *(hulled wheat)*
100 ml (½ cup) beer
700 ml (3 cups) water
salt
25 g (1 oz) butter
30 g (1 oz) hazelnuts *(without skins)*

For the baked plums, heat the oven to 120 °C (250 °F). Rinse the plums in cold water, halve and remove the stones. Transfer the plums to an ovenproof dish, add the lemon juice and sprinkle over the rose petals, sugar and finely grated lemon zest. Bake the plums for 15–20 minutes until they are soft and tender but still hold their shape and have some 'bite'.

Take the plums out of the oven and turn them carefully over in the juices that have come from the cooking. Leave the plums to soak for 20–30 minutes before serving. Alternatively, the baked plums can be made several days in advance and kept in the fridge.

For the porridge, bring the oats, spelt, beer, water and salt to the boil in a pan. Heat gradually for 5–6 minutes until the mixture boils and forms a thick porridge. Stir in the butter and mix well to make the porridge soft and creamy. Add a little sugar to taste, if needed.

Serve the porridge straight away, while still warm and smooth, with the baked plums and some plum juice from the dish, and sprinkle with the roughly chopped hazelnuts.

breakfast juice

WITH CARROT, STRAWBERRY, GINGER AND PINK GRAPEFRUIT

SERVES 4

10 carrots

10 strawberries

3 pink grapefruit

10–15 g (0.25–0.5 oz) ginger

Wash the carrots and strawberries and slice off the tops. Peel the grape-fruit and ginger.

Press the carrots, strawberries, ginger and grapefruit through a juicer to make a beautiful 'orange' juice.

Transfer the juice to a jug with a few ice cubes and serve straight away.

baked grapefruit

WITH SPICES, LENTILS, RED ONION, FETA, MINT AND BASIL

SERVES 4

100 g (3.5 oz) dried green lentils
salt and freshly ground pepper
50 ml (3 tbsp) olive oil
4 pink grapefruit
2 cinnamon sticks
5 bay leaves
4 cardamom pods
15 cumin seeds
3 star anise
1 red onion
1 tsp acacia honey
35 ml (2 tbsp) apple cider vinegar
50 g (2 oz) feta
½ bunch basil
½ bunch mint

Put the lentils in a pan and rinse them with cold water. Drain and add fresh water so it covers the lentils and bring to the boil. Boil the lentils for 30–35 minutes until they are tender but still retain their shape and bite.

Meanwhile heat the oven to 180 °C (360 °F).

Drain the lentils and season with salt, freshly ground pepper and a little olive oil. Put to one side to cool.

Peel and halve the grapefruit widthways. Place the grapefruit in an oven-proof dish cut side up, sprinkle over all the spices and drizzle with olive oil. Put the dish in the oven and bake the grapefruit for 10–12 minutes until soft and lightly browned.

Peel, halve and thinly slice the red onion. Transfer the strips of onion to a bowl together with the honey, vinegar and a little salt and leave to marinate for 10 minutes.

Serve the baked grapefruit topped with the cooked green lentils, the red onion and the feta, garnished with basil and mint. Serve for breakfast or as part of a brunch.

toasties

WITH MORTADELLA, GRASS-FED CHEESE AND KIMCHI

SERVES 4

8 slices good sourdough bread

4 large slices mortadella

50 g (2 oz) grass-fed organic cheese
  (or other good hard cheese)

2 tbsp mustard

100 g (4 oz) kimchi *(ready-made jar or tin)*

Spread one side of each slice of bread with mustard, lay the mortadella on top of 4 slices, then distribute thin slices of cheese over the mortadella.

Next add a good spoonful of kimchi and finally place another slice of bread on top to make a sandwich ready for toasting.

Toast the filled sandwiches in a sandwich maker for 2–3 minutes until the bread is nice and crispy and the cheese has melted.

Cut each toastie into two and serve while warm.

buttermilk pancakes

WITH FRIED APPLES AND CINNAMON SUGAR

SERVES 4

PANCAKES

4 eggs

200 g (1¼ cups) plain flour

½ vanilla bean

zest of 1 organic lemon

250 ml (1 cup) milk

250 ml (1 cup) buttermilk

40 g (1.5 oz) butter

CINNAMON SUGAR

50 g (2 oz) sugar

1 tbsp ground cinnamon

FRIED APPLES

4 apples

35 g (2 tbsp) honey

20 g (1 oz) butter

juice of 1 organic lemon

For the pancakes, beat the eggs in a bowl and stir in the flour, mixing until smooth. Split the vanilla bean and scrape the seeds into the pancake mix. Grate the lemon zest and add to the bowl. Add the milk and buttermilk and keep stirring to make a smooth and runny pancake batter.

In a small pan, melt 30 g (1 oz) butter and add to the pancake batter while stirring thoroughly. Place the pancake batter in the fridge for 30 minutes to rest and take on the flavour of the vanilla and lemon.

Then warm a pan, melt the rest of the butter and let it bubble a little before pouring a spoonful of pancake batter into the pan. Fry for approx. 1 minute until golden. Flip the pancake over and fry for a further 30 seconds, then remove the pancake from the pan. Repeat until all of the pancake batter has been used up. Keep the pancakes warm until ready to serve with the fried apples and cinnamon sugar.

For the cinnamon sugar, mix the sugar and cinnamon together in a bowl. Set aside.

For the fried apples, peel the apples, remove the cores and cut into large cubes. In a pan, heat the honey until it begins to caramelize. Add the butter and the apples and fry for 1–2 minutes so the apples absorb the flavour of the butter and honey. Squeeze the lemon juice over the apples and fry for a further 1 minute so the lemon juice and honey cook into the apples.

Remove the apples from the pan and serve with the warm pancakes and cinnamon sugar.

baking

breakfast buns

MAKES 15 BUNS

20 g (1 oz) fresh yeast

100 ml (½ cup) natural yoghurt

500 ml (2 cups) cold water

1 tbsp salt

200 g (7 oz) stone-milled finely sifted
   Øland wheat flour *(alternatively, any
   heirloom flour or normal organic wheat flour)*

400 g (14 oz) organic plain flour

Stir the yeast, yoghurt and water together. Add a little of the flour before the salt, then the rest of the flour, stirring with a wooden spoon until you have a cohesive dough. (If you add the salt first, you risk breaking down some of the yeast's leavening ability.) The dough should be very soft and pliable, but still a little wet.

Put the dough in a bowl or plastic tub, cover with a lid or tea towel and refrigerate. Let the dough rise in the refrigerator for at least 12 hours, preferably overnight.

The next day, take the dough out of the refrigerator and let it stand for 1 hour on the kitchen worktop to reach room temperature.

Heat the oven to 250°C (480°F), with a baking tray inside. Turn the dough out onto a floured surface and divide into buns with a spatula or palette knife, then gently lift the buns onto a sheet of baking paper. Take the heated baking tray out of the oven and slide it under the baking paper with the buns. Put the tray back in the oven.

Bake the buns for 10–12 minutes until they are golden on the surface and nice and crisp. Allow to cool a little on a wire rack before serving.

seeded rye bread

WITH FENNEL AND LIQUORICE

MAKES 2 LOAVES

200 ml (¾ cup) buttermilk
600 ml (2½ cups) cold water
150 ml (¾ cup) beer
20 g (1 tbsp) salt
10 g (2 tsp) fresh yeast
300 g (1¾ cups) cracked rye kernels
225 g (1½ cups) flax seeds
150 g (¾ cup) sunflower seeds
115 g (¾ cup) sesame seeds
250 g (9 oz) plain flour
300 g (10 oz) rye flour
1 tsp liquorice powder
1 tsp whole fennel seeds *(ground)*

Blend all the ingredients in a mixer for approx. 10 minutes to form a good cohesive dough.

Split the dough into two halves and transfer into 2 small greased tins lined with baking paper to make it easier to remove the bread from the tin when baked.

Cover the dough with clingfilm and refrigerate for a minimum of 12 hours, preferably for 24 hours, so the flavour of the seeds develops. The dough can be left in the fridge for up to 5 days, so you can just take it out on the day you need it.

Bake the dough at 180°C (360°F) for 1 hour until cooked through and golden.

Transfer the two breads from the tins to a wire rack and leave to rest for at least 20 minutes before serving. The bread needs to cool a little before it can be cut into slices.

crispbread

WITH DRIED FLOWERS

MAKES 4 FULL
BAKING TRAYS

500 ml (2 cups) water
250 g (9 oz) plain flour
80 g (½ cup) flax seeds
140 g (¾ cup) sesame seeds
70 g (½ cup) sunflower seeds
70 g (½ cup) pumpkin seeds
100 ml (½ cup) grapeseed oil
1 handful dried marigolds
1 handful dried blue cornflowers
sea salt

Bring the water to the boil. Mix all the dry ingredients (except the flowers) in a bowl. Then add the mixture and grapeseed oil to the boiling water, stirring with a wooden spoon until the mixture is smooth and even.

Heat the oven to 150°C (300°F). Now spoon a blob of the mixture onto a smallish rectangle of baking paper, cover with a second rectangle of baking paper and spread the mixture out until it is approx. 1–2 mm thick, either by running your hands over the surface of the paper or using a rolling pin.

Remove the top piece of baking paper and sprinkle the crispbread with some of the dried flowers and some sea salt. Do the same with the rest of the crispbread mixture.

Transfer the baking sheet to a baking tray and bake the mixture until it is golden and crunchy. This should take 40–45 minutes, but keep an eye on the crispbread while it is baking to make sure it does not get too dark.

focaccia

WITH ASPARAGUS AND WILD GARLIC FLOWERS

MAKES 1 FOCACCIA

700 ml (3 cups) cold water

200 ml (¾ cup) buttermilk

20 g (1 oz) fresh yeast

500 g (17 oz) organic plain flour

300 g (11 oz) wholemeal Øland wheat
flour (alternatively, any heirloom flour or
normal organic wholewheat flour)

20 g (1 oz) sea salt

100 ml (½ cup) olive oil

10 green asparagus spears

1 handful wild garlic flowers

Mix the cold water and buttermilk together and stir in the yeast. Add both types of flour and the salt, and knead well with a spoon until you have a smooth and cohesive dough. Leave the dough to rise for approx. 12 hours in the fridge, covered with a cloth.

Grease a baking tray (approx. 40 × 32 cm / 15 × 12 in) with a little of the olive oil. Transfer the dough to the baking tray, pressing it gently so that the dough completely covers the base of the tray.

Cut off the ends of the asparagus spears and rinse the spears to remove any dirt. Spread the whole asparagus spears and the wild garlic flowers over the surface of the dough. Finally, drizzle the bread with olive oil and sprinkle with sea salt. Leave the dough to rise in the tray for ½–1 hour.

Bake the focaccia at 230 °C (445 °F) for approx. 15 minutes. Reduce the heat to 200 °C (390 °F) and bake for a further 20 minutes until crisp and golden. Leave the baked focaccia to cool on a wire rack so that it keeps its crispy crust.

Serve as part of a main meal.

rosemary buns

WITH OLIVE OIL

MAKES 10–12 BUNS

25 g (1 oz) fresh yeast

500 ml (2 cups) cold water

100 ml (½ cup) lager

1 tbsp salt

300 g (11 oz) Italian 'Tipo 00' flour

400 g (14 oz) organic plain flour

200 ml (7 oz) olive oil

5 sprigs rosemary

sea salt

In a bowl, stir the yeast, water and lager together. Add a little of the flour before the salt, then the rest of the flour, stirring with a wooden spoon until you have a cohesive dough. (If you add the salt first, you risk breaking down some of the yeast's leavening ability.) The dough should be soft and pliable, without sticking to your fingers when you work it. Put the dough in a bowl or plastic tub, cover with a lid or tea towel and refrigerate. Let the dough rise in the refrigerator for at least 12 hours, preferably overnight.

The next day, take the dough out of the refrigerator and let it stand for 1 hour on the kitchen worktop to reach room temperature. Then divide the dough into 10–12 pieces and roll them flat, tucking the sides under to create tight little buns. Place the buns on a floured surface, well spaced apart, and leave to rise for 1–1½ hours until they have doubled in size.

Now press down the middle of each bun and gently push out the sides to form a depression in the middle of approx. 7–8 cm (3 in) in diameter and a crust all the way around. Then gently lift the buns and place them on a piece of baking paper, leaving them to rise for a further 15–20 minutes.

Meanwhile, heat the oven to 230 °C (450 °F), with a baking tray inside. Drizzle the buns with olive oil and sprinkle with rosemary leaves and some sea salt. Take the baking tray out of the oven and slide it under the baking paper. Put the tray back in the oven and bake for 12–15 minutes until the buns are golden and lightly toasted on the surface. Remove from the oven and allow to cool on a wire rack before serving.

Serve with lunch or dinner. If you make more pastries than you can eat on one day, you can enjoy them again the next day. They taste great heated in the oven or in a toaster.

rhubarb and marzipan cake

WITH LEMON THYME

150 g (5 oz) softened butter

150 g (5 oz) sugar

150 g (5 oz) marzipan

3 medium-sized eggs

50–75 g (2–3 oz) flour

3–4 stalks rhubarb

30 g (1 oz) cane sugar

10 sprigs lemon thyme

Heat the oven to 170 °C (340 °F). Stir the butter, sugar and marzipan together to form a soft mass. Add the eggs one at a time (or break them all together and add a little at a time) until you have a smooth cake mixture. Fold in the flour and stir well.

Grease a springform cake tin with a little soft butter, then sprinkle the inside of the tin with some sugar so that it sticks all the way around the tin. This helps the baked cake to slip from the tin and gives it a nice caramelized surface. Spoon or pour the cake mixture into the tin.

Cut the leaves off the rhubarb stalks, then rinse the stalks in cold water. Cut the stalks into 1–2 cm (½–1 in) pieces and place in a bowl. Toss the pieces in the cane sugar. Spread the rhubarb pieces across the top of the cake mixture, pressing a few pieces down into the mixture if you wish.

Rinse the lemon thyme in cold water, roughly chop and sprinkle over the cake. Bake the cake for 30–35 minutes until cooked through and golden.

Remove the cake from the oven and allow to cool a little before serving with yoghurt, whipped cream or ice cream. The cake can be made the day before serving as it retains moisture and freshness well.

cinnamon swirls

WITH BLACKCURRANTS

MAKES 20 SWIRLS

DOUGH

50 g (2 oz) fresh yeast

200 ml (¾ cup) lukewarm water

40 g (2 oz) sugar

200 ml (¾ cup) whole milk

120 g (4 oz) butter

a little salt

700 g (25 oz) plain flour

2 eggs

a little milk for glazing

FILLING

200 g (7 oz) softened butter

200 g (7 oz) sugar

4 tbsp cinnamon *(ground)*

25 g (1 oz) freeze-dried blackcurrants

For the dough, pour the water into a bowl and stir in the yeast. Then add the rest of the dough ingredients. Knead the dough until it is smooth and even. Cover the bowl with a cloth and leave the dough to rise for 30–45 minutes at room temperature.

Make the cinnamon mixture while the dough is rising. Whisk the butter, sugar and cinnamon together to form a well-blended mixture. Leave to stand for the flavour to develop.

Heat the oven to 210 °C (410 °F). On a floured surface, roll the dough into a rectangle of approx. 50 × 30 cm (20 × 12 in) and spread the cinnamon butter over the dough in a thin layer. Then sprinkle over the crushed freeze-dried blackcurrants. Now fold one side of the dough over so that ⅓ of the dough surface is still 'showing'. Then fold this part of the dough over the two folded layers so you have a smaller rectangle of dough with three layers.

Cut the dough perpendicular to the folds into 20–25 strips. Taking one strip at a time, twist it with both hands in opposite directions. Place the twists on a baking tray and coil them into 'swirls', taking care not to place them too close together, as they will rise and expand while baking. Tuck the ends of each swirl underneath. Cover with a tea towel and leave to rise for a further 30 minutes.

Remove the tea towel and brush each swirl with milk. Bake in the middle of the oven for 12–14 minutes. They are ready when they are lovely and golden on the surface and make a slightly hollow sound when tapped. Remove the swirls from the oven and leave to cool on a wire rack. Enjoy while still warm, or save for later. The swirls can also be frozen and re-heated another day.

chocolate muffins

MAKES 12–14 MUFFINS

2 eggs
170 g (6 oz) sugar
100 g (4 oz) dark chocolate
140 g (5 oz) coconut flour
50 g (2 oz) flour
2 tsp vanilla sugar
125 g (4.5 oz) melted butter
muffin tins/cases

Heat the oven to 200 °C (390 °F). Whisk the eggs and sugar together until they are thoroughly mixed.

Chop up the chocolate and, in a separate bowl, mix with the coconut flour, flour and vanilla sugar, then stir into the egg mixture. Finally add the melted butter and blend it all together to form an even batter.

Divide the muffin mixture equally between the cases. Bake in the oven for 15–17 minutes until the muffins are cooked through and golden on top, but still 'spongy' in the middle. Allow the muffins to cool before eating.

The muffins can be made a day or two before they are eaten as they will stay nicely spongy and moist thanks to the coconut flour.

meringue kisses

WITH SPRUCE AND HIBISCUS

MAKES 10–12 MERINGUES

500 g (17 oz) sugar

100 ml (½ cup) water

whites of 8 medium-sized eggs

10 fresh or pickled spruce tops *(if you don't have spruce tops, you can use a little chopped rosemary, lemon thyme or lemon balm)*

2 tbsp hibiscus powder

In a saucepan, combine the water and 400 g (14 oz) of the sugar to make a syrup. Heat the syrup until it reaches a temperature of 120 °C (250 °F); it is a good idea to use a sugar thermometer! Keep a close eye on the mixture so that it does not reduce by too much and start turning brown.

Whisk the egg whites with the remaining 100 g (3 oz) of sugar in a blender or with an electric whisk until the mixture is slightly stiff.

When the temperature of the syrup has reached 120 °C (250 °F), add the chopped spruce tops and remove the pan from the heat. Slowly pour the syrup (in a thin drizzle) into the egg whites while the blender or whisk is still going. Whisk until the mixture stands up in stiff peaks and has completely cooled. This will take around 5–7 minutes.

Heat the oven to 70–80 °C (160–175 °F). Add half of the hibiscus powder to the mixture, folding it in gently so that it makes a pattern in the meringue. Now use a dough scraper to drop 10–12 spoonfuls of meringue onto a sheet of baking paper, trying to make tiny 'mountains' each a slightly different shape.

Sprinkle the meringues with the rest of the hibiscus powder and bake in the oven for 6–7 hours until they are crisp and dry. They can be baked overnight, if necessary (as long as you don't oversleep!). Alternatively, the meringues can be baked at 100–120 °C (200–250 °F) for 2–3 hours, but keep an eye on them so they don't become too dark.

Eat the baked meringues on their own or serve as a dessert with fresh berries and ice cream.

on the
beach

For me, a Danish summer is long, light evenings and being together as a family. We really value spending time together on the Danish shores, swimming in the warm water, fishing from the beach and catching crabs from the jetties, or foraging for edible things and cooking them over an open fire we have made ourselves.

crab bisque

WITH FENNEL, PEAS AND HERBS

You will need an old cast iron pot.

1 kg (2 lbs) live shore crabs

50 ml (3 tbsp) olive oil

2 shallots

2 cloves garlic

5 sprigs thyme

2 tomatoes

1 fennel

100 ml (½ cup) apple juice *(natural or cloudy, unfiltered and unsweetened)*

300 ml (1¼ cups) good cider

2 litres (4 pints) of water

salt, sugar, vinegar and freshly ground pepper

500 g (18 oz) fresh peas

½ bunch tarragon

bread to serve

Shore crabs are ideal for soup – they give a great flavour. Kill the crabs as quickly as possible. This can be done by cutting them through with a sharp knife. Lay a crab hard shell side down on a chopping board. Hold it in place with a knife by pressing the blade against the crab's belly plate, then push down so that you cut through its head quickly. Please note that different countries have different regulations regarding the killing of crabs, and you should check that you are using an approved method.

Repeat the process for the remaining crabs and place the crabs together with their juices in a bowl.

Heat the pot until it is really hot, add the oil and roast the crabs for 2–3 minutes until they take on a nice colour.

Peel the shallots and garlic and add to the pot, along with the thyme, tomatoes and the tops of the fennel (save the fennel bulb and the peas for later). Add the apple juice and cider, bring to the boil and let the liquid reduce by half.

Then add enough water to just cover the crabs. Bring back to the boil and cook for another 20 minutes.

Remove the soup from the heat and let it rest for 10 minutes before sieving it into a bowl. Return the soup to the pot and let it reduce slightly. Season with salt, sugar, vinegar and freshly ground pepper.

Finely slice the fennel bulb and add to the soup with the freshly shelled peas. Drizzle with a little olive oil and sprinkle with chopped tarragon.

Serve straight away with a hunk of good bread.

COUSCOUS

WITH SEAWEED-GRILLED WHITE ASPARAGUS, ELDERFLOWER,
SWEET CICELY AND SHALLOTS

SERVES 4

250 g (9 oz) couscous
salt and freshly ground pepper
100 ml (½ cup) olive oil
8 white asparagus spears
2 large handfuls fresh bladderwrack
    or other edible seaweed (optional)
3–4 fresh elderflower heads
2 shallots
4 sprigs sweet cicely (chervil or flat leaf parsley
    may also be used)
juice and zest of 1 organic lemon

Put the couscous in a saucepan and rinse with cold water. Discard the water and add fresh water so that it covers the couscous by about 2 cm (1 in). Add a little salt and olive oil. Bring to the boil and cook the couscous until all the water has been absorbed and the couscous is tender.

Remove the pan from the heat and let the couscous stand for 5–7 minutes. Season to taste with extra salt and freshly ground pepper.

Peel the asparagus and cut off the ends. Then wrap the spears in the fresh bladderwrack and elderflowers and place on a grill pan. The seaweed serves to 'steam' the asparagus and protects it from burning, so it can also be grilled over an open fire. If you can't get bladderwrack or any other fresh edible seaweed, you should blanch the white asparagus a little, to ensure that it is tender before grilling.

Grill the asparagus in the seaweed for approx. 6–7 minutes until it is tender and slightly charred. Take the asparagus off the grill, remove any remaining seaweed and elderflowers (most of which will have 'burned' away in any case), then cut it into small pieces and add to the couscous.

Peel, halve and finely chop the shallots. Chop the sweet cicely and add to the couscous together with the shallots. Stir well and season with the finely grated zest and juice of the lemon, olive oil, salt and freshly ground pepper.

Serve with grilled mackerel (see page 92).

seaweed flatbread

WITH SEA SALT, HERBS, FLOWERS AND OLIVE OIL

MAKES 8–10 FLATBREADS

10 g (2 tsp) dried seaweed *(dulse or bladderwrack)*

10 g (2 tsp) fresh yeast

200 ml (¾ cup) warm water

100 ml (½ cup) dark beer

300 g (11 oz) plain flour

5 g (1 tsp) sea salt

150 g (5 oz) finely ground Øland wheat flour *(alternatively, any heirloom flour or normal organic wheat flour)*

100 ml (½ cup) olive oil

1 handful herbs and edible flowers

Grind the seaweed with a pestle and mortar.

In a bowl, dissolve the yeast in the water and beer, then add a little plain flour before adding the salt, as otherwise the salt may 'kill' some of the yeast cells. Add the rest of the flour (both types) as well as the ground seaweed. Then knead the dough well until it no longer sticks to the sides of the bowl or your fingers and is smooth and pliable. Leave the dough to rest until it has doubled in size (about 1 hour).

Turn the dough out onto a floured surface and divide it into 8–10 small balls. Roll each ball out into thin a flatbread. Drizzle with a little olive oil and sprinkle with the herbs, flowers and a little salt.

Toss each bread in a hot pan or toast over an open fire for 1–2 minutes on each side until golden. Drizzle with a little extra oil while cooking, if necessary.

Serve with soup.

whole grilled mackerel

WITH MIXED HERBS

4 whole mackerel

salt and freshly ground pepper

50 ml (3 tbsp) olive oil

2 handfuls mixed herbs

Clean and gut the mackerel, rinsing the fish in cold water to wash away any blood. Season with a little salt and freshly ground pepper and drizzle with half of the olive oil.

Grill the mackerel with the herbs on a high heat for 4–5 minutes on each side until they are golden on the outside but still juicy in the middle.

Transfer the mackerel from the grill pan to a plate. Season with a little extra salt and olive oil.

The grilled mackerel goes well with couscous (see page 86) or a salad of pointed cabbage (see page 94).

pointed cabbage salad

WITH FROMAGE FRAIS AND SALTED GOOSEBERRIES

SERVES 4

½ pointed cabbage

100 g (4 oz) fresh gooseberries *(or frozen)*

sea salt and freshly ground pepper

1 tsp sugar

35 ml (2 tbsp) apple cider vinegar

50 ml (3 tbsp) olive oil

200 ml (¾ cup) fromage frais

100 ml (½ cup) natural yoghurt

Heat the oven to 120°C (250°F). Roughly chop the cabbage, rinse in cold water and dry thoroughly. Place the gooseberries in an ovenproof dish, sprinkle with 1 tsp salt and 1 tsp sugar and bake for 10–12 minutes so they are just warm and slightly soft.

Take the gooseberries out of the oven and add the vinegar and oil to make a warm dressing. Leave the dressing to stand for 10–15 minutes to allow the flavour to develop before serving.

Put the fromage frais and yoghurt in a bowl, add a little salt and freshly ground pepper and combine to form a smooth cream.

Spoon the fromage frais mixture onto a plate, layer the cabbage over the top and drizzle with the gooseberry dressing.

Serve with grilled mackerel (see page 92).

wild rose lemonade

MAKES 1.5 LITRES
OR 10 GLASSES

1 litre (2 pints) water
400 g (14 oz) cane sugar
10 organic lemons
3 handfuls wild rose petals
ice cubes

In a saucepan bring the water, sugar and the juice of 9 lemons to the boil. Cut the last lemon into slices and add to the pan. Bring back to the boil and add the rose petals. Then remove the pan from the heat and leave the mixture to cool for 40–45 minutes.

You can either sieve the lemonade before serving or leave the rose petals in it. Add a little extra water and serve with lots of ice.

The lemonade can be made several days before serving and will keep for 2–3 weeks in the refrigerator.

toasted marshmallows

WITH STRAWBERRIES AND BISCUITS

MAKES 30–40 PIECES

500 g (17 oz) sugar

100 ml (½ cup) water

½ vanilla bean

whites of 3 large eggs

10 leaves gelatine

icing sugar

10 fresh locally grown strawberries

long wooden skewers or thin branches

60–80 rich tea biscuits/Marias

Bring the sugar and water to the boil with the vanilla bean to form a syrup. Beat the egg whites until they are stiff and stir into the syrup.

Soak the gelatine leaves according to the packet instructions and add to the syrup and egg white mixture. Stir until the mixture is lukewarm and the gelatine has dissolved. Spread the mixture onto a sheet of grease-proof paper and leave to cool.

Cut the cooled mixture into 30–40 pieces of a suitable size and turn each piece in icing sugar so that they don't stick together.

Rinse the strawberries and remove the leaves. Cut the strawberries into thin slices and place them on a platter with the biscuits.

Now toast the marshmallows on a skewer over an open fire. As soon as they are nice and caramelized on the surface but still sticky in the middle, sandwich them between 2 biscuits and 1–2 slices of strawberry and eat with your fingers.

eggs

scrambled eggs

WITH FRIED ASPARAGUS, TARRAGON AND BUCKWHEAT

SERVES 4

8 eggs
100 ml (½ cup) milk
salt and freshly ground pepper
50 ml (3 tbsp) olive oil
12 green asparagus spears
2 tbsp whole buckwheat groats
5 sprigs tarragon

Crack the eggs into a bowl, add the milk, salt and freshly ground pepper and beat well to form an even mixture.

In a frying pan, heat a little oil, then add the egg mixture. Heat gently while stirring with a wooden spoon or a dough scraper, turning the eggs around as the mixture settles on the pan to make light and fluffy scrambled eggs. Transfer the scrambled eggs from the pan to a bowl and keep warm.

Rinse the asparagus in cold water, cutting off and discarding the ends. Dry thoroughly. Cut each asparagus spear into 2–3 pieces.

Wipe the pan clean, then add fresh oil and fry the asparagus on a high heat for 1–2 minutes until lightly golden but still crunchy. Season with salt and freshly ground pepper.

Take the asparagus from the pan, and add the buckwheat. Toast the buckwheat for a few minutes on a low heat until it is golden and starting to release its aroma. Remove the buckwheat from the pan.

Divide the scrambled eggs between the plates and top with the asparagus, buckwheat, some picked tarragon and a little olive oil. Serve straight away for breakfast or lunch.

egg salad on waffles

WITH CAULIFLOWER AND PICKLED RED ONION

SERVES 4

EGG SALAD

4 eggs

35 ml (2 tbsp) Greek yoghurt

1 tbsp mustard

1 tsp curry powder

25 g (1 oz) gherkins

salt and freshly ground pepper

¼ cauliflower

1 red onion

35 ml (2 tbsp) apple cider vinegar

2 sprigs basil

WAFFLES

250 g (9 oz) plain flour

2 tsp baking powder

a little salt

300 ml (1¼ cups) whole milk

100 ml (½ cup) water

150 ml (⅔ cup) tonic water

110 g (4 oz) melted butter

30 g (1 oz) freshly grated parmesan

butter to grease the waffle iron

For the egg salad, carefully lower the eggs into a saucepan of water, making sure they are fully immersed. Bring to the boil and cook for 6 minutes. Remove the pan from the heat and run cold water over the eggs. Peel and roughly chop the eggs, then transfer to a bowl. Add the yoghurt, mustard, curry powder, chopped gherkins, salt and freshly ground pepper and mix gently.

Rinse the cauliflower and cut into very thin slices using a mandolin slicer. Put half into the egg salad and stir. Put the other half into a bowl of cold water. Season the salad to taste with extra curry powder, salt and freshly ground pepper as needed.

Peel, halve and thinly slice the red onion. In a separate bowl, combine the red onion slices with the vinegar and a little salt. Stir well and set aside for 15 minutes while the flavour develops and the onions lose their sharp taste but still retain a little bite.

Take the cauliflower out of the water and dry thoroughly.

For the waffles, combine the flour, baking powder and salt in a bowl. Add the milk, water and tonic water and stir everything well. Pour in the melted butter, add the grated parmesan and stir until you have a smooth waffle batter. Leave the batter to rest for 1 hour before cooking on a hot waffle iron. Remember to grease the waffle iron with a little butter before pouring in the batter. Cook the waffles for approx. 2–3 minutes until crisp and golden. Repeat until all the batter has been used up.

Serve the warm waffles topped with the egg salad, some pickled red onions, the remaining cauliflower flakes and some roughly chopped basil.

fried eggs

WITH FRIED RAPESEED FLOWERS AND PARMESAN

2 handfuls organic rapeseed flowers
   (alternatively, green asparagus or broccolini)
50 ml (3 tbsp) extra virgin olive oil
4 eggs
sea salt and freshly ground pepper
40 g (2 oz) freshly grated parmesan

Rinse the rapeseed flowers in cold water. Remember to be very thorough as there may be tiny insects hidden in the flowers (it is important that you use organic rapeseed flowers). Put a pan on a medium heat and let it get really warm.

Add a little oil to the pan, crack the eggs into it and fry for 1–2 minutes until the egg white is fried and set but the yolk is still soft and runny. Season with sea salt and freshly ground pepper.

Transfer the fried eggs from the pan onto 4 plates. Add a little more oil to the pan and fry the rapeseed flowers for 1–2 minutes until tender but still crisp. Season with sea salt and freshly ground pepper.

Take the rapeseed flowers from the pan and arrange on top of the fried eggs. Drizzle with a little olive oil and sprinkle with freshly grated parmesan. Eat while the eggs and flowers are hot. Serve with good bread.

omelette

WITH POTATOES AND PEAS

SERVES 4

6 eggs
200 ml (¾ cup) milk
salt and freshly ground pepper
300 g (10.5 oz) cooked new potatoes
35 ml (2 tbsp) extra virgin olive oil
200 g (7 oz) peas *(shelled weight)*
½ bunch fresh basil
30 g (1 oz) pea shoots

Heat the oven to 180 °C (350 °F). Crack the eggs into a bowl, add the milk, salt and freshly ground pepper and whisk well.

Cut the cooked potatoes into small pieces. Pour the oil into a heated pan with a metal handle, add the potato pieces and fry for 3–4 minutes until golden. Season with salt and pepper.

Add half of the peas and the chopped basil to the pan with the potatoes, then pour the egg mixture over the top. Fry until the egg mixture has just set on the bottom of the pan, then transfer the pan to the oven. Cook the omelette for approx. 15 minutes until firm and golden.

Remove the pan from the oven (remember that the pan handle will be hot!), then transfer the omelette to a plate. Arrange the pea shoots and the rest of the peas on top of the omelette, and season with a little salt and freshly ground pepper. Serve with good bread.

egg-fried rice

WITH BEANS, CHILLI AND BASIL

SERVES 4

300 g (10.5 oz) green beans
50 ml (3 tbsp) olive oil
½ fresh red chilli *(deseeded)*
600 g (21 oz) cooked rice
4 eggs
50 ml (3 tbsp) soy sauce
35 ml (2 tbsp) oyster sauce
salt and freshly ground pepper
5 sprigs basil

Rinse the beans in cold water and trim off both ends. Cut the beans into 3–4 pieces and place in a bowl.

In a wok or large frying pan, heat the oil. Finely chop the chilli and add to the pan. Fry on a low heat for 1 minute. Add the beans and fry for 2 minutes until slightly browned. Season with salt.

Add the cooked rice to the pan. Mix everything well and fry the rice for 3–4 minutes. Crack the eggs into the rice, stirring while frying so that the rice and eggs are well combined. Season with soy sauce, oyster sauce, salt and freshly ground pepper.

Pick the basil leaves off the stalks. Chop half the leaves and stir into the rice. Make sure everything is mixed well, then transfer the mixture to a bowl. Garnish with the rest of the basil leaves and serve straight away.

Enjoy as a main meal for lunch or as a side dish. This is a good way to use up rice left over from the day before.

soft-boiled eggs

WITH YELLOW SPLIT PEA PUREE AND COTTAGE CHEESE

SERVES 4

150 g (5 oz) yellow split peas

1 tbsp dried chamomile flowers

100 ml (½ cup) extra virgin olive oil

50 ml (3 tbsp) apple cider vinegar

salt and freshly ground pepper

2 eggs

100 g (½ cup) cottage cheese

1 handful garden nasturtium leaves

For the puree, rinse the peas in cold water and add them to a saucepan. Cover with water. Add the chamomile flowers and bring to the boil. Cook the peas for 35–40 minutes until tender. Drain the cooked peas, retaining some of the cooking water to adjust the consistency of the puree if necessary.

In a blender, combine the warm peas, oil, vinegar, salt and freshly ground pepper. Blend to a smooth puree, adding some of the retained cooking water if necessary, so that the puree has the right consistency. Leave the puree to cool and season to taste with a little extra vinegar, salt and pepper.

Bring a pan of water to the boil. Carefully lower the eggs into the boiling water and cook for 5–5½ minutes. When the time is up, immerse the eggs immediately in cold water so that the cooking stops and the egg yolks stay soft and runny. Peel the eggs and cut them in half.

For each serving, drop a spoonful of the yellow split pea puree into a bowl and top with half a soft-boiled egg and a good spoonful of cottage cheese. Season with a little salt and freshly ground black pepper. Garnish with the garden nasturtium leaves and serve as a light breakfast or lunch.

toast

WITH POACHED EGG AND SPICY CHICKPEAS

SERVES 4

100 g (3.5 oz) chickpeas
100 ml (½ cup) olive oil
1 clove garlic
½ fresh red chilli *(deseeded)*
1 tbsp ras el hanout
salt and freshly ground pepper
1 tin chopped peeled tomatoes
35 ml (2 tbsp) vinegar
4 eggs
4 slices sourdough bread
5 sprigs thyme

Soak the chickpeas in cold water and leave to soften for 24 hours. Transfer the chickpeas to a saucepan, draining off any remaining water. Then add fresh water so that it covers the chickpeas by about 3–4 cm and bring to the boil. Cook the chickpeas for 40–45 minutes until tender, then remove the pan from the heat and transfer the chickpeas to a bowl.

Put the pan back on the heat and add some oil. Peel and chop the garlic and finely chop the chilli, then add the garlic and chilli to the pan and sauté lightly without browning. Add the chickpeas and the ras el hanout, mix well and season with salt and freshly ground pepper. In a separate bowl, blend the chopped peeled tomatoes with a stick blender to make a tomato sauce, then add to the chickpeas. Bring to the boil, then turn the heat down and cook for approx. 20 minutes until the tomato sauce has thickened and coated the chickpeas. Season with a little extra salt and freshly ground pepper if needed.

For the poached eggs, bring a saucepan of water to the bowl, add a little vinegar and reduce the heat so the water just simmers. Crack an egg into a cup and season with a little salt and freshly ground pepper. Now swirl the simmering water round with a spoon to create a small whirlpool, pour the egg carefully into the whirlpool so that the egg white gathers around the yolk. Poach the egg for 3½–4 minutes, then lift it gently out of the pan with a slotted spoon. Immerse the egg in cold water. Repeat the same steps for the rest of the eggs.

In a frying pan, fry the slices of sourdough bread in olive oil until crisp and golden on both sides. Arrange the slices of bread on a plate, cover with a good spoonful of the spiced chickpeas and top with a poached egg. Season with thyme leaves, a few drops of olive oil, sea salt and freshly ground pepper. Serve immediately for breakfast or as a light lunch.

lunch

pea puree

WITH RADISH, FETA AND CRISPY FLATBREAD

SERVES 4

200 g (7 oz) shelled peas *(500–600 g (1 lb)*
  in whole weight; frozen peas can also be used)
30 g (1 oz) almonds
100 ml (½ cup) olive oil
35 g (2 tbsp) ricotta
20 g (1 oz) freshly grated parmesan
4 sprigs mint
sea salt and freshly ground pepper
zest of ½ organic lemon
4 radishes
3–4 flatbreads
25 g (1 oz) feta

Blanch the peas in boiling water for 30 seconds, then drop them straight into cold water to stop them cooking.

Toast the almonds in a dry pan until lightly golden.

In a food processor, blend the peas with 50 ml (3 tbsp) of the olive oil, the toasted almonds, ricotta, parmesan and half the mint until you have a coarse puree. Season to taste with salt, pepper and a some finely grated lemon zest. Transfer the pea puree from the food processor to a bowl or plate.

Cut the roots and tops off the radishes and, using a mandolin slicer, finely slice the radishes lengthways. Put the slices into a bowl of cold water so that they become extra crunchy and curl a little.

Meanwhile, cut the flatbreads into large triangles and fry them in olive oil until crisp and golden. Remove from the pan and sprinkle with sea salt while still warm.

Drain the radishes and allow them to dry completely. Arrange the pea puree and warm flatbreads on plates, top with radishes and crumbled feta, then garnish with the remaining mint leaves.

The pea puree can be made in advance and kept in the fridge, and taken out when needed.

fermented radishes

MAKES APPROX. 1.5 LITRES

You will need a 1.5-litre preserving jar.

550 g (1 lb) radishes

50 g (2 oz) spring onions or shallots

1 handful wild garlic flowers *(optional,
    if they are in season)*

30 g (1 oz) salt

½ litre (2 cups) water

Clean the radishes thoroughly, but avoid scrubbing them. Slice off the tops and stems, weigh them and put half into the preserving jar. Peel and roughly chop the shallots or spring onions. Add to the jar with the radishes and wild garlic flowers. Then fill the jar with the rest of the radishes.

Make your pickling brine by adding the salt to 100 ml (½ cup) boiling water. Stir well so that the salt dissolves, then add the remaining 400 ml (1½ cups) cold water; the brine should then be at roughly room temperature.

Pour the brine over the radishes so that they are completely covered. Make sure to leave a 3–4 cm (1–1.5 in) space at the top of the jar, close it and leave in a cool place for the contents to ferment. This should take 5–7 days at 18–20 °C (65–68 °F). If the temperature is higher than this, the fermenting will be quicker; if it's colder, it will take longer.

The jar should be opened every day to release the carbon dioxide the fermentation process creates. Taste the radishes after 5 days or sooner, depending on the temperature. When the radishes are ready, put the jar in the fridge. The radishes will keep in the fridge for up to 3 weeks (after that they will be too fermented).

Serve the fermented radishes as a snack, with a sandwich or in a salad.

ribollita

WITH BACON, PARMESAN AND PARSLEY

100 g (3.5 oz) white beans

2–3 carrots

1 fennel

200 g (7 oz) celery

2 cloves garlic

2 shallots

50 g (2 oz) good dry cured bacon

50 ml (3 tbsp) extra virgin olive oil

5 sprigs thyme

salt and freshly ground pepper

1½ litres (6¼ cups) vegetable stock

zest of 1 organic lemon

5 sprigs flat-leaf parsley

40 g (2 oz) freshly grated parmesan

Soak the beans in cold water and leave to soften for 24 hours. The next day, put the soaked beans in a pan, cover with fresh water and bring to the boil. Cook the beans for 30–35 minutes until they are tender but still have some bite. Take the pan off the heat and keep the beans warm in the cooking water.

Rinse and peel the carrots, fennel and celery, then roughly chop into cubes and transfer to a bowl. Peel and finely chop the garlic and shallots. Chop the bacon into small cubes.

Add some oil to a frying pan and sauté the bacon, garlic and shallots for 2–3 minutes until the bacon and shallots have browned. Add the chopped thyme and vegetables and let them fry a little in the oil until they soften slightly. Season with salt and freshly ground pepper, then add the stock and bring to the boil. Let the soup cook for 15 minutes until the vegetables are tender and the soup has absorbed all the flavours.

Add the white beans and cook for a further 5 minutes. Finally, season with finely grated lemon zest and some extra salt and pepper if needed.

Serve the soup with chopped parsley and grated parmesan on top. You can make the soup the day before and warm it up when you're hungry.

pizza

WITH POTATO, MASCARPONE AND BASIL

SERVES 4

DOUGH

15 g (0.5 oz) fresh yeast

300 ml (1¼ cups) warm water

500 g (17 oz) plain flour (*preferably Italian; 'Tipo 00' is good*)

15 g (2 tsp) salt

35 ml (2 tbsp) extra virgin olive oil

PIZZA

4 potatoes, the size of a chicken egg

4 pieces dough

100 g (3.5 oz) mascarpone

75 g (3 oz) freshly grated parmesan

5 sprigs basil

50 ml (3 tbsp) good olive oil

sea salt

For the dough, dissolve the yeast in the warm water in a mixing bowl. Add the flour, salt and olive oil while stirring with an electric mixer on a low speed setting. Keep mixing until you have a nice smooth dough. Then remove the dough and knead it by hand for 4–5 minutes until it is stretchy and firm. Leave the dough to rise for 45–60 minutes.

Heat the oven to 250 °C (480 °F) with a baking tray inside.

Peel and thinly slice the potatoes using a mandolin slicer or a very sharp knife. Put the slices in a bowl of cold water and leave them for 10–15 minutes to remove excess potato starch and so the potatoes don't soften and turn brown.

Divide the dough into 4 pieces, each piece roughly the size of a tennis ball, then on a floured surface roll the dough out very thinly (approx. 2–3 mm in thickness).

Divide the mascarpone between the 4 bases and spread onto the dough in a thin layer. Distribute the potato slices over the bases and sprinkle with parmesan. Roughly chop the basil and sprinkle over the pizzas.

Put the pizzas into the oven on the hot baking tray and bake for 8–10 minutes until they begin to bubble and turn golden on top, with a crispy base and crust. Take the pizzas out of the oven and serve straight away with a drizzle of olive oil, some extra basil and a little sea salt.

samosas

WITH POTATO, PEAS AND SPICES

MAKES 12–14 SAMOSAS

400 g (14 oz) small potatoes

1 onion, finely chopped

1 clove garlic, finely chopped

50 ml (3 tbsp) olive oil

2 tsp cumin

10 g (0.25 oz) ginger

1 tsp ras el hanout

1 pinch dried chilli

1 tsp coriander

200 g (7 oz) fresh peas *(frozen peas can also be used)*

juice and zest of 1 organic lemon

1 packet filo pastry

salt and freshly ground pepper

For the filling, wash the potatoes thoroughly and put in a pan. Cover with salted water and bring to the boil. Cook for 15–20 minutes until the potatoes are tender, then drain them and mash them roughly with a fork.

Peel and finely chop the onion and garlic. In a pan, heat 2 tsp of oil and sauté the onion and garlic. Add the spices and stir well. Sauté for a further 1 minute. Add the mashed potatoes and peas, and season with finely grated lemon zest and juice, salt and pepper. Leave the filling to cool.

Heat the oven to 200°C (390°F). Cut the filo pastry lengthways into rectangles approx. 15–20 cm (6–8 in) wide, and brush the surface with oil. Spoon approx. 2 tbsp of the filling in one corner and fold the pastry over so that it seals around the filling and forms a triangle. Brush with oil, sprinkle with a little sea salt and place the samosas on a sheet of baking paper. Cook in the oven for 12–15 minutes until crisp and golden.

Remove the samosas from the oven and eat while they are still crunchy and warm. A tasty and healthy snack for the kids, which can also be served cold as part of a packed lunch.

yellow split pea dhal

WITH HERBS AND CRISPY RYE BREAD

SERVES 4

DHAL

2 red onions

salt and freshly ground pepper

50 ml (3 tbsp) apple cider vinegar

25 g (1 oz) fresh ginger

1 fresh red chilli

100 ml (½ cup) olive oil

3 star anise

5 bay leaves

1 cinnamon stick

5 cardamom pods

400 g (14 oz) yellow split peas

3 sprigs mint

2 sprigs bronze fennel

CRISPY RYE BREAD

¼ of a loaf of day-old rye bread

30 ml (2 tbsp) olive oil

sea salt

A larger amount of crispy ryebread can be made several days in advance and kept in an airtight container. It's a delicious snack for children when they get home from school.

For the dhal, peel, halve and finely slice the red onion. Put half of the onion in a bowl and sprinkle with a little salt and 20 ml (1 tbsp) of vinegar and mix well. Leave the onion to stand and marinate for 30 minutes so it loses some of its sharpness but keeps a little bite.

Peel and finely slice the ginger. Rinse and finely chop the chilli, keeping the seeds. Put 50 ml (3 tbsp) olive oil in a pan, add the rest of the onion, the ginger, chilli and spices and sauté for 2–3 minutes to release all the flavours and aromas. Add the split peas and sauté for a further 1–2 minutes so that the peas absorb the flavours of the spices. Season with a little salt and freshly ground pepper.

Add enough water to cover the peas by approx. 2–3 cm (1 in) and bring to the boil. Cook the peas for 30–35 minutes on a low heat, stirring occasionally so the peas don't stick to the bottom of the pan.

When the peas are cooked well but still have the texture of peas, you will have a smooth dhal. Season to taste with salt, freshly ground pepper, vinegar and olive oil.

For the crispy rye bread, heat the oven to 150°C (300°F). Cut the rye bread into thin slices. (Putting the bread in the freezer for a few minutes can make it easier to cut it into very thin slices.) Place the slices of bread on a sheet of baking paper, drizzle with olive oil and sprinkle with a little sea salt. Bake the rye bread slices for 8–10 minutes until golden and crispy all over, taking care not to overcook them, when they can taste a little bitter. Remove the rye bread from the oven and leave to cool.

Serve the dhal in bowls or deep plates, garnished with the mint and fennel, with crispy rye bread.

crispy chickpeas

WITH PICKLED ONIONS AND SWEET CICELY

SERVES 4

PICKLED ONIONS

3 red onions

4 banana shallots

300 ml (1½ cups) apple cider vinegar

100 g (4 oz) sugar

1 tsp salt

5 whole black peppercorns

10 fennel seeds

CRISPY CHICKPEAS

200 g (7 oz) chickpeas

50 ml (3 tbsp) olive oil

sea salt

sweet cicely *(alternatively, you can use chervil or flat-leaf parsley)*

For the pickled onions, peel the onions and banana shallots and cut into quarters.

In a pan, bring the vinegar, sugar, salt and spices to the boil to make a pickle brine. Add the onions and cook for 1 minute. Then take the pan off the heat.

Transfer the onions and the brine to a bowl or jar and leave to stand for at least 4 hours, preferably a couple of days, before using. The pickled onions can be kept refrigerated until needed.

For the crispy chickpeas, soak the chickpeas in cold water for 24 hours. Drain the water and rinse the chickpeas thoroughly, then transfer them to a pan and cover with water. Bring to the boil and cook for 35–40 minutes until the chickpeas are tender. Remove the pan from the heat and pour off any excess water.

Warm some olive oil in a frying pan and fry the chickpeas over a medium heat until golden and crispy. Season with sea salt.

Take the chickpeas out of the pan and serve with pieces of pickled onion and fresh sweet cicely as a light afternoon snack.

chicken skewers

WITH CARROT AND TAHINI DRESSING, PICKLED CARROTS AND DUKKAH

SERVES 4

DRESSING
6 carrots
juice and zest of 1 organic lemon
2 tbsp tahini
1 tsp acacia honey
salt and freshly ground pepper
50 ml (3 tbsp) olive oil

PICKLED CARROTS
2 carrots
100 ml (½ cup) apple cider vinegar
35 ml (2 tbsp) honey
salt

For the carrot and tahini dressing, peel the carrots and slice off the tops and roots. Roughly chop the carrots and drop into a pan, just covering them with salted water. Cook the carrots for 8–10 minutes until they are tender but still crunchy. Drain the water from the carrots, keeping approx. half of the cooking water to dilute the dressing to the right consistency later.

Blend the carrots with the finely grated zest and juice of the lemon, tahini, honey, salt and freshly ground pepper. Add the olive oil and a little bit of the cooking water to make a smooth dressing. Season the dressing to taste with a little extra of the ingredients if needed, as the sweetness of the carrots can vary greatly depending on the season.

Transfer the dressing to a bowl so it is ready to serve. The dressing can be made in a larger quantity and kept in the fridge, so the children can help themselves when they get home from school and eat it with whatever they like.

For the pickled carrots, peel the carrots and slice off the tops and roots. Then slice the carrots lengthways into very thin strips using a mandolin slicer. Put the carrot strips into a bowl.

In a pan, boil the vinegar, honey and some salt, then pour the hot brine over the carrots. Leave to soak for 15–20 minutes before serving. The pickled carrots can also be made in a larger portion and kept in the fridge.

DUKKAH

50 g (2 oz) hazelnuts

50 g (2 oz) sesame seeds

50 g (2 oz) sunflower seeds

50 g (2 oz) pumpkin seeds

1 tbsp whole coriander seeds

1 tbsp whole cumin

1 tsp dried chilli flakes

sea salt and freshly ground pepper

1 tbsp dried marigold

1 tbsp dried blue cornflowers

CHICKEN

2 chicken breasts

30 ml (2 tbsp) olive oil

sea salt and freshly ground pepper

4 wooden skewers

For the dukkah, toast all the spices, seeds and nuts on a dry pan for 2–3 minutes until they begin to pop and release aromas. Remove from the pan and crush with a pestle and mortar to a coarse mixture. Add the dried flowers and mix everything well. Serve the dukkah in a bowl. It can also be kept in an airtight container for later use.

Cut the chicken breasts into cubes of approx. 2 × 2 cm (1 × 1 in) and put in a separate bowl. Turn in some olive oil, salt and freshly ground pepper. Thread the chicken pieces onto the skewers and leave to marinate for 10 minutes.

Warm a grill pan and grill the chicken skewers over a high heat for 3–4 minutes on each side until beautifully charred but juicy in the middle. Remove the chicken skewers from the pan and serve with the dressing, pickled carrots and dukkah.

spinach pancakes

WITH PRAWNS, YOGHURT AND PICKLED SHALLOTS

SERVES 4

SPINACH PANCAKES
125 g (4.5 oz) baby spinach
300 ml (1¼ cups) milk
3 eggs
200 g (7 oz) plain flour
sea salt and freshly ground pepper
40 g (2 oz) butter

FILLING
2 shallots
juice and zest of 1 organic lemon
1 tbsp acacia honey
sea salt and freshly ground pepper
200 g (7 oz) whole fresh prawns
50 ml (3 tbsp) olive oil
200 ml (¾ cup) Greek yoghurt
100 g (3.5 oz) baby spinach

For the pancakes, rinse the spinach and put it in a blender with the milk. Blend until the milk is uniformly green. Beat the eggs in a bowl and stir in with the spinach milk, adding the flour a little at a time to make a completely even, smooth batter. Season with salt and pepper.

In a small pan, melt 30 g (1 oz) butter and add to the pancake batter while stirring thoroughly.

Heat a frying pan, add the rest of the butter and then a good spoonful of pancake batter. Fry the pancake for approx. 30 seconds on each side until it turns a nice colour. Repeat until all the pancake batter has been used up. Keep the pancakes warm while you make the filling.

For the filling, peel, halve and finely chop the shallots and put in a bowl with the juice and finely grated zest of the lemon, honey, salt and freshly ground pepper. Stir well and leave to marinate for 10 minutes.

Shell the prawns and put them in a bowl. Heat some oil in a pan and fry the prawns on a high heat for 30 seconds to 1 minute until they are slightly browned and becoming crispy. Season with salt and freshly ground pepper and remove from the pan.

Serve the pancakes warm with the fried prawns and the pickled shallots, Greek yoghurt and baby spinach. The pancakes can be made in advance and warmed when required.

rye bread sandwich

WITH GRILLED ASPARAGUS, MOZZARELLA AND HOMEMADE CHILLI SAUCE

SERVES 4

CHILLI SAUCE

(Makes 1 jar, can be kept for 2–3 weeks in the fridge)

10 g (0.25 oz) fresh ginger

10 fresh red chillies

30 ml (2 tbsp) olive oil

30 g (1 oz) sugar

salt and freshly ground pepper

100 ml (½ cup) apple cider vinegar

1 tin peeled chopped tomatoes

SANDWICH

16 green asparagus spears

8 slices rye bread

50 ml (3 tbsp) olive oil

salt and freshly ground pepper

2 pcs fresh mozzarella

4 sprigs tarragon

2 sprigs mint

For the chilli sauce, peel and thinly slice the ginger. Rinse the chillies and snip off the tops, chop them roughly and add to a pan with the olive oil and ginger. Sauté on a low heat for 2–3 minutes until soft and beginning to release an aroma.

Add the sugar, salt and pepper and allow to caramelize slightly. Add the vinegar and let the mixture boil until it is reduced by half. Then add the tomatoes and bring back to the boil. Cook on a low heat for 20–25 minutes until the mixture has combined into a thick sauce.

Transfer the sauce to a blender and blend to make a smooth sauce. Season to taste with salt, pepper and a little extra sugar and vinegar if necessary. The sauce should be strong but also have a good balance of sweet and sour flavours. Transfer the sauce to a jar or bowl and set aside.

For the rye bread sandwich, cut the ends off the asparagus spears and rinse in cold water. Allow to dry thoroughly. Toast the rye bread slices on a grill pan with a little olive oil until crisp and golden. Remove the bread slices and add fresh oil to the grill pan. Grill the asparagus for 1–2 minutes on each side until they are charred and tender but still have some bite. Season with salt and pepper, then remove from the pan.

Put a slice of rye bread on each of 4 plates. Divide the asparagus so that there are 4 pieces on each slice of bread. Tear the mozzarella into small pieces and distribute over the asparagus. Rinse the herbs and sprinkle the leaves onto the mozzarella. Finally, drizzle with homemade chilli sauce, olive oil, salt and pepper. Place another piece of rye bread on top of the filling and enjoy as a satisfying lunch sandwich.

flatbread toasties

WITH GRILLED VEGETABLES AND PARMESAN

SERVES 4

2 courgettes

1 aubergine

salt and freshly ground pepper

3 cloves garlic

10 sprigs thyme

100 ml (½ cup) olive oil

2 red peppers

juice and zest of 1 organic lemon

4 flatbreads

½ bunch basil

50 g (2 oz) freshly grated parmesan

Heat the oven to 220°C (430°F). Wash the courgettes and aubergine, slice them and turn the slices in some salt, freshly ground pepper, roughly chopped garlic, thyme and some olive oil. Leave to marinate for 15 minutes.

Wash the peppers and put them in an ovenproof dish. Drizzle with olive oil and sprinkle with salt. Bake the peppers in the oven for 15 minutes until they are well browned and slightly soft. If necessary, turn the peppers occasionally while cooking to make sure they are evenly baked. Take the peppers out of the oven and let them cool before deseeding and peeling.

Roughly chop the peppers and transfer the pieces to a bowl. Season with salt, freshly ground pepper and olive oil.

On a heated grill pan, grill the slices of courgette and aubergine under a high heat for 1–2 minutes on each side, so they take on a beautiful pattern of char marks. Remove the slices from the pan and add to the bowl with the peppers. Mix them together and season with the finely grated lemon zest and juice, extra salt and freshly ground pepper.

Fill a flatbread with the vegetables, basil leaves and grated parmesan, and toast the sandwich in a toaster or sandwich maker for 2–3 minutes until it is nice and crispy and the parmesan has melted into the vegetables. Cut the toastie into small pieces and eat while still warm.

You can make the vegetables the day before or in a larger portion to keep in the fridge for when you fancy a sandwich.

in the
orchard

I remember how as a child I loved to sit under the fruit trees at my aunt's and uncle's plantation on the island of Tåsinge and just eat fruit all day long until I got a stomach ache! My children have inherited this fondness – they enjoy climbing apple trees, picking apples and eating them straight from the branch. There is no tastier way to eat fruit, especially apples.

apple galette

WITH RICOTTA, THYME, SUNFLOWER AND LEMON

MAKES 12 SERVINGS

1 sheet puff pastry

50 g (3 tbsp) ricotta

4 apples

5 sprigs thyme

1 sunflower head

35 g (1 oz) sugar

juice of 1 organic lemon

Heat the oven to 220 °C (430 °F). Make a circle of puff pastry by placing a plate measuring approx. 28 cm (11 in) on top of the pastry sheet and cutting around it with a knife. (Store the excess pastry in the fridge or freezer for another time.) Place the circle of pastry on a baking sheet lined with greaseproof paper. Spoon the ricotta onto the middle of the pastry and spread outwards, leaving a border of approx. 2–3 cm (1 in) all the way around.

Rinse the apples and cut them into very thin slices using a mandolin slicer. Arrange the apple slices closely together on top of the ricotta, starting from the outside and working towards the centre for a neat finish. Sprinkle the apples with the chopped thyme, sunflower leaves, sugar and lemon juice.

Bake the galette in the oven for 18–20 minutes until the pastry is cooked through and golden and the apples are slightly caramelized on the surface. Keep an eye on the galette while it is cooking, turning it round if necessary to ensure an even bake.

Remove the galette from the oven and allow to cool a little before cutting into slices and serving while it is still warm.

The galette can be made in advance and eaten cold or re-heated a little before serving.

apple and blackberry jam

MAKES 1 LARGE BOWLFUL

4 apples *(Discovery or Ingrid Marie)*
150 g (5 oz) blackberries
100 g (4 oz) sugar
juice and zest of 1 organic lemon

Rinse the apples in cold water and remove the cores (keep the cores for preserving – see page 174). Then dice the apples into approx. 1 × 1 cm (0.5 × 0.5 in) cubes.

In a saucepan bring the diced apples, blackberries, sugar, lemon juice and finely grated lemon zest to the boil with the lid on. Simmer over a low heat for 8–10 minutes until the apples and blackberries are soft but the apples retain their shape and texture. Remember to stir the jam while it is cooking so that it doesn't burn. Remove the pan from the heat and transfer the jam to a bowl to cool.

When it has cooled, taste the jam and add some more lemon juice and sugar if necessary. The acidity/sweetness of the apples can vary greatly depending on the time of year and variety of apple.

Serve with good bread.

The jam will keep for 2–3 weeks in the fridge – but don't expect it to last that long!

cloudy apple juice

WITH TONIC AND SEA BUCKTHORN

10 apples
100 g (½ cup) sea buckthorn
200 ml (1 cup) tonic
ice cubes

Rinse the apples in cold water and squeeze them through a juicer along with the sea buckthorn to make a beautiful orange-coloured juice.

Pour the juice into a jug, add the tonic and lots of ice. Serve straight away as a refreshing afternoon or evening drink.

preserved apple cores

15–20 apple cores
500 g (18 oz) coarse salt

Put the apple cores in a jar and cover with the salt. Close the lid and shake the jar until all the cores are covered with salt.

Leave the jar on your kitchen worktop or on a shelf for at least 3 weeks before using. In fact, the apple cores may be left for 5–6 months – the longer the better!

Use them as an alternative to preserved lemon in dressings (see page 176), as a stuffing for whole grilled fish or as a marinade for roast chicken (see page 218).

baked beetroot

WITH A DRESSING OF PRESERVED APPLE CORES, CHICKPEAS AND MINT

SERVES 4

100 g (3.5 oz) chickpeas
100 ml (½ cup) olive oil
50 ml (3 tbsp) apple cider vinegar
salt and freshly ground pepper
1 kg (2 lbs) fresh beetroot
300 g (11 oz) salt
2 preserved apple cores *(see page 174)*
  or 1 whole fresh apple
35 ml (2 tbsp) acacia honey
5 sprigs mint

Put the chickpeas in a bowl, cover with water and leave to soak for 24 hours. The next day, drain the chickpeas and transfer to a pan. Add enough fresh water to cover the chickpeas and bring to the boil. Cook the chickpeas for 30–35 minutes until they are tender but still have a little bite.

Heat the oven to 170 °C (340 °F). Transfer the cooked chickpeas from the pan to a bowl, add 2 tbsp olive oil, 2 tbsp apple cider vinegar, a little salt and freshly ground pepper, stir well and leave them to marinate.

Slice the tops off the beetroot and wash away any soil. Dry with a paper towel. Place the beetroot in an ovenproof dish and cover with the salt. Bake in the oven for 70–80 minutes until soft and tender.

When they are cooked, let the beetroot cool, then remove them from the dish, peel with a vegetable knife and cut into small pieces. Divide onto 4 plates.

Rinse the salt from the preserved apple cores and blend with the rest of the olive oil and vinegar, the honey and some freshly ground pepper to make a smooth dressing. Pour the dressing into a bowl.

Spoon the cooked chickpeas over the beetroot, add a good drizzle of the apple core dressing and finally garnish with some mint leaves. Serve with good bread, as a stand-alone vegetable dish or as an accompaniment to meat or fish.

apple salad

WITH FENNEL, SMOKED MACKEREL AND HEMP SEEDS

SERVES 4

2 fennel bulbs

2 apples

1 smoked mackerel

100 ml (½ cup) fermented milk *(e.g. kefir)*

30 ml (2 tbsp) olive oil

35 ml (2 tbsp) apple cider vinegar

20 ml (1 tbsp) acacia honey

salt and freshly ground pepper

2 tbsp hemp seeds

1 handful garden nasturtium leaves

Slice off the shoots and roots of the fennel bulbs and rinse the fennel in cold water. Finely slice the fennel using a mandolin slicer or a sharp knife and transfer to a bowl.

Wash the apples and remove the cores (keep them for preserving, see page 174). Slice the apple into very thin wedges and add to the bowl with the fennel.

Remove the skin and bones from the smoked mackerel and break the fish into large pieces. Add to the apples and fennel.

Pour the fermented milk into another bowl and season with the olive oil, vinegar, honey, salt and freshly ground pepper. Mix well to make a dressing.

Stir the salad and dressing together and season to taste with a little extra salt and pepper, if needed.

Serve the salad in a large bowl or divided between 4 plates, garnished with hemp seeds and nasturtium leaves, accompanied by good bread. Eat as a lunchtime salad or starter.

pasta

pasta dough

SERVES 8

To make your own pasta, you will need a pasta machine; then it's very simple.

200 g (7 oz) durum wheat flour
200 g (7 oz) Italian 'Tipo 00' flour
salt
3 egg yolks
2 whole eggs

Heap the two types of flour and a little salt on a surface and make a well in the middle. Add the 3 egg yolks and 2 whole eggs into the well. Carefully combine everything to make a firm and pliable dough. Add a little water if it seems too dry.

Wrap the dough in cling film and put it in the fridge to rest for 30–60 minutes before dividing it into smaller pieces and rolling it through your pasta machine – how thin you make the pasta is a question of taste. I prefer it to be rolled quite thin.

Then attach the cutter to the machine and run the dough through it again, which will cut the dough into the desired shape – for example, spaghetti/tagliolini, tagliatelle or pappardelle.

When making ribbon pasta, it is a good idea to sprinkle the ribbons with a little flour and twirl them into small 'nests' on a baking sheet or tray until needed.

spaghetti alle vongole

WITH WILD GARLIC

SERVES 4

500 g (1 lb) clams *(or cockles)*
1 shallot
100 ml (½ cup) olive oil
200 ml (¾ cup) white wine
300 g (10.5 oz) fresh spaghetti
salt and freshly ground pepper
half a dozen wild garlic leaves and
   a few flowers *(cleaned)*

Bring a pan of salted water to the boil.

Rinse the clams with cold water to remove all sand and dirt. Check that the clams are closed. If any are open, give them a light tap and see if they close up; if not, discard them. Transfer the clams to a sieve to dry.

Peel, halve and finely chop the shallot. In a large pan, add half the oil and lightly sauté the shallot for a couple of minutes until translucent and the oil has been absorbed. Add the clams and white wine and stir well. Put the lid on the pan and steam the clams for 2 minutes until they open. Take care not to steam them for too long, or they will become tough and dry. Take the pan off the heat but leave the lid on to keep the clams warm.

Cook the spaghetti in the pan of salted water for 2 minutes (or 8–9 minutes if using dry spaghetti) until al dente. Transfer the spaghetti to a sieve and drain off all the water.

Add the spaghetti to the clams, season with the remaining 50 ml olive oil, the roughly chopped wild garlic leaves, a little salt and freshly ground pepper, and stir well so that the spaghetti absorbs some of the moisture from the clams and everything is mixed well.

Spoon into deep plates, making sure everyone gets some clams and sauce. Garnish with some more wild garlic leaves and flowers.

Serve straight away while the pasta and clams are still warm.

ravioli

WITH MUSHROOMS AND PARMESAN

SERVES 4

300 g (10 oz) mixed mushrooms
1 clove garlic
35 ml (2 tbsp) olive oil
salt and freshly ground pepper
50 g (3 tbsp) ricotta
50 g (2 oz) freshly grated parmesan
juice and zest of 1 organic lemon
400 g (14 oz) fresh pasta
5 stalks of flat leaf parsley

Clean the mushrooms and dice 250 g (½ lb) of them. Save the remaining 50 g (2 oz) to fry and add as a garnish later. Peel and finely chop the garlic. Add a little oil to a pre-heated pan and sauté the garlic with the diced mushrooms until browned and soft. Season with salt and freshly ground pepper. Remove from the heat and leave to cool a little.

In a food processor, blend the mushrooms, ricotta and half the grated parmesan to make a thick mushroom paste. Season to taste with salt, pepper and lemon juice and freshly grated zest. Transfer the mushroom paste to a bowl and put it in the fridge to cool completely and set.

Make the pasta (described on page 188), but instead of cutting it with your pasta machine, cut it by hand into two matching rectangles. Using the blunt edge of a circular cookie cutter, mark out 12–16 circles on one rectangle of pasta. Place a spoonful of the mushroom filling in the middle of each circle. Brush the pasta with a little water around the edge of the filling, then place the other rectangle of pasta on top. Gently press the pasta around the spoonfuls of filling to form a tight seal all the way around. With a sharp knife, cut the ravioli into squares so that the filling is right in the middle of each piece.

Bring a pan of salted water to the boil, add the ravioli and cook for 3–4 minutes until the pasta is al dente and the filling is warm through.

Fry the remaining mushrooms in a little oil until brown and soft. Season with salt and freshly ground pepper. Rinse and finely chop the parsley.

Transfer the ravioli from the water into deep plates, distribute the mushrooms on top of each serving and sprinkle with the remainder of the grated parmesan and the chopped parsley. Serve straight away.

spaghetti with meatballs

IN TOMATO SAUCE

SERVES 4

TOMATO SAUCE

2 onions

2 cloves garlic

50 ml (3 tbsp) olive oil

10 sprigs thyme, finely chopped

800 g (2 tins) peeled chopped tomatoes

salt and freshly ground black pepper

MEATBALLS

3–4 tbsp oatmeal

50 ml (¼ cup) milk

500 g (1 lb) minced beef

salt and freshly ground pepper

1 onion

2 cloves garlic

2 eggs

25 g (1 oz) freshly grated parmesan

50 ml (3 tbsp) olive oil

SPAGHETTI

1 tbsp salt

400 g (14 oz) fresh spaghetti

100 g (3.5 oz) freshly grated parmesan

1 bunch basil

For the tomato sauce, peel and finely chop the onion and garlic and sauté in olive oil until the onions are translucent. Add the thyme and tomatoes. Bring to the boil, then put a lid on the pan and leave the sauce to simmer for 15 minutes. Season to taste with salt and freshly ground pepper. Blend the tomato sauce with a stick blender until smooth. Remove the pan from the heat and set to one side while you make the meatballs.

For the meatballs, combine the oatmeal and milk in a bowl and put to one side to let the oatmeal absorb the milk. In another bowl, break up the minced beef and stir with a little salt and freshly ground pepper. Peel and finely chop the onion and garlic and add to the beef, stirring well. Add the eggs and the grated parmesan and continue to stir well to make a thick meat mixture. Season with a little extra salt and freshly ground pepper if needed. Leave the meat to rest for 15–20 minutes before frying. Meanwhile, heat the oven to 180 °C (360 °F).

In a frying pan, heat a little olive oil. Using a spoon, shape the meat mixture into small round balls, about the size of ping-pong balls, and fry on a high heat for 2–3 minutes so the meatballs have a nice crust but are still quite juicy in the middle. Continue until all the meat mixture has been used up. Transfer the cooked meatballs to an ovenproof dish and pour over the tomato sauce. Put the dish in the oven for 15 minutes so that the meatballs absorb some of the tomato sauce and become firm.

Cook the spaghetti in the pan of salted water for 2 minutes (or 8–9 minutes if using dry spaghetti) until al dente. Drain and transfer to a bowl.

Remove the meatballs in tomato sauce from the oven. Serve straight away with the spaghetti, topped with freshly grated parmesan and chopped basil.

penne

SERVES 4

300 g (10 oz) fresh peas *(or frozen)*
½ fresh red chilli, seeds removed
50 ml (3 tbsp) olive oil
300 g (10 oz) penne *(dry pasta)*
50 g (2 oz) freshly grated parmesan
salt and freshly ground pepper
1 pc mozzarella
2 sprigs tarragon

Shell the peas into a bowl. Finely chop the chilli.

Bring a pan of salted water to the boil. Cook the penne in the boiling water for 8–9 minutes.

Meanwhile, in a pan, sauté the chilli in the oil on a low heat for 1–2 minutes so the oil absorbs some of the flavour of the chilli. Then sauté the shelled peas in the chilli oil on a low heat for 1–2 minutes so they stay firm and green.

Now drain the pasta and transfer to the pan with the peas and the chilli. Add the parmesan, salt and pepper and stir well.

Spoon the pasta into deep plates or bowls. Break the mozzarella into small pieces and arrange on top. Garnish with the tarragon, a little olive oil and freshly ground pepper. Serve straight away before the mozzarella melts completely over the pasta.

cannelloni

WITH FRIED CAVOLO NERO, RICOTTA AND HAZELNUTS

SERVES 4

TOMATO SAUCE

1 onion

2 cloves garlic

50 ml (3 tbsp) olive oil

5 sprigs thyme, finely chopped

400 g (1 tin) peeled chopped tomatoes

salt and freshly ground black pepper

FILLING

400 g (14 oz) cavolo nero *(Tuscan/black kale)*

35 ml (2 tbsp) olive oil

100 g (3.5 oz) hazelnuts, roughly chopped

salt and freshly ground pepper

250 g (1 cup) ricotta

2 eggs

25 g (1 oz) freshly grated parmesan

fresh nutmeg, for grating

CANNELLONI

8–12 (1 pack) fresh lasagne sheets

50 g (2 oz) freshly grated parmesan

salt and freshly ground pepper

For the tomato sauce, peel and finely chop the onion and garlic and sauté in olive oil until the onions are translucent. Add the thyme, followed by the tomatoes. Bring to the boil, then put a lid on the pan and leave the sauce to simmer for 15 minutes. Season to taste with salt and freshly ground pepper. Remove the pan from the heat and keep the sauce warm.

For the filling, shred the cavolo nero into small pieces and rinse in cold water. Dry thoroughly.

Add some olive oil to a pre-heated pan and lightly toast the chopped hazelnuts until golden. Transfer half the toasted hazelnuts to a bowl. Add two-thirds of the cavolo nero to the pan, stirring well so that the hazelnuts do not burn and the cavolo nero wilts a little. Season with salt and freshly ground pepper. Remove the cavolo nero and hazelnuts from the pan and leave to cool a little. Then stir in the ricotta together with the eggs and grated parmesan, and season with salt, freshly ground pepper and some finely grated nutmeg.

For the cannelloni, heat the oven to 175°C (350°F). Spread half the tomato sauce onto a greased ovenproof dish. Spoon some cavolo nero and ricotta mixture onto a sheet of pasta and roll it up around the filling. Place it in the dish. Repeat with the rest of the pasta sheets and filling until everything is used up. Spread the rest of the tomato sauce over the stuffed cannelloni. Sprinkle half the grated parmesan over the top and bake in the oven for 20 minutes until the pasta is tender and the parmesan is gratinated.

Now fry the rest of the cavolo nero in some olive oil. Season with salt and pepper. Serve the cannelloni garnished with the fried cavolo nero, the remaining toasted hazelnuts and a little freshly grated parmesan.

veggie pasta bolognese

SERVES 4

1 onion

2 cloves garlic

50 ml (3 tbsp) olive oil

250 g (½ lb) mixed mushrooms

10 sprigs thyme

75 g (3 oz) chopped sun-dried tomatoes in oil

400 g (1 tin) peeled chopped tomatoes

200 ml (¾ cup) red wine

300 g (10 oz) dry pasta

salt and freshly ground pepper

50 g (2 oz) grated parmesan

a few edible flowers *(optional)*

Peel and chop the onion and garlic. Add 35 ml (2 tbsp) of the olive oil to a pan and sauté the onion and garlic on a low heat for a couple of minutes.

Clean the mushrooms and mince them in a food processor until they are finely chopped. Add the mushrooms to the pan and sauté them for 3–4 minutes until soft and brown.

Chop the thyme and add most of it (keep 1 tbsp for garnishing the dish later), along with the chopped sun-dried tomatoes and red wine, and sauté for a further 1–2 minutes.

Blend the peeled chopped tomatoes to make a completely smooth sauce and add to the mushroom mixture, stirring well. Season with salt and freshly ground pepper. Let the mushroom and tomato sauce cook for 20–25 minutes until it reduces to make a thick vegetarian bolognese.

Bring a pan of water to the boil. Add the pasta and cook for 8–9 minutes until al dente. Drain well.

Add the sauce to the pasta and stir well. Season to taste with a little extra salt and freshly ground pepper. Serve straight away in deep plates and season with lots of parmesan, a little fresh thyme and edible flowers.

pasta carbonara

SERVES 4

100 g (3.5 oz) pancetta
35 ml (2 tbsp) olive oil
4 eggs
100 g (3.5 oz) freshly grated parmesan
salt and freshly ground pepper
300 g (10.5 oz) fresh pasta

Remove the rind and any cartilage from the pancetta and cut it into cubes. In a sauté pan (sauteuse) fry the pancetta cubes in a little olive oil over a low heat so the fat slowly melts and mixes with the olive oil. The pancetta should be ready in approx. 3–4 minutes – cooked but not to a crisp.

Bring a pan of salted water to the boil.

Crack the eggs and separate the whites and the yolks. Put the yolks in a bowl and the whites in the fridge to use another day (for example, for meringues, marshmallow or a 'white' omelette). Add most of the grated parmesan to the egg yolks. Keep the remaining parmesan to serve with the pasta later. Season the egg yolks and parmesan with salt and freshly ground pepper.

Add the pasta to the pan of water and boil for 2 minutes (or 8–9 minutes if using dry pasta) until al dente. Remove the pasta from the water and transfer to the sauteuse with the pancetta so that it retains a little of the cooking water to mix with the pancetta fat.

Now pour the egg yolks and parmesan into the warm pasta and stir well so that the egg yolk and parmesan combine with the water and pancetta fat to make a lovely creamy sauce coating the pasta. Season with some extra salt and freshly ground pepper.

Stir a few more times and spoon straight into deep plates, making sure everyone gets some pancetta and sauce. Sprinkle the remaining parmesan on top and serve.

dinner

veggie balls

WITH HERBS, COUSCOUS AND MINT YOGHURT

SERVES 4

VEGGIE BALLS

1 cauliflower

2 baking potatoes

1 shallot

1 clove garlic

4 eggs

30 g (1 oz) chopped hazelnuts

1 tsp paprika

1 tsp chilli powder

1 tbsp baking powder

½ bunch mint

½ bunch flat-leaf parsley

salt and freshly ground pepper

50 ml (3 tbsp) oil *(grapeseed or rapeseed)*

COUSCOUS

300 g (10.5 oz) couscous

juice and zest of 1 organic lemon

salt and freshly ground pepper

50 ml (3 tbsp) olive oil

½ bunch flat-leaf parsley

MINT YOGHURT

300 ml (1¼ cup) Greek yoghurt

½ bunch mint

50 ml (3 tbsp) olive oil

salt and freshly ground pepper

For the veggie balls, rinse the cauliflower and remove the outer leaves. Grate into a bowl. Peel and grate the potatoes into the bowl. Peel and finely chop the shallot and garlic and add to the cauliflower and potato. Add the eggs, hazelnuts, spices, baking powder and chopped herbs (saving some to garnish the balls later), and combine everything well together to make a dense paste. Season to taste with salt and pepper, and leave to rest for 15–20 minutes for the flavours to develop.

Heat the oil in a pan and, using a spoon, form the mixture into balls and fry them for approx. 4–6 minutes, turning them regularly so that they are nice and golden all over. Transfer the balls to a plate and warm them in the oven just before serving.

Put the couscous in a pan and add water to cover it by 3–4 cm (1–2 in). Season with the finely grated lemon zest, lemon juice, salt and 25 ml (1½ tbsp) olive oil. Bring to the boil and cook for 7–8 minutes until the water has been absorbed and the couscous is tender. Remove the pan from the heat and leave the couscous to infuse for 3–4 minutes.

Meanwhile, rinse the parsley and allow to dry thoroughly before finely chopping the leaves. Add the rest of the olive oil to the couscous and season to taste with some extra salt and freshly ground pepper, if needed. Transfer to a bowl and sprinkle the chopped parsley on top.

For the mint yoghurt, blend the yoghurt, mint, olive oil, salt and freshly ground pepper to make a smooth light green yoghurt. Transfer the mint yoghurt to a bowl and sprinkle some chopped mint on top.

Serve the veggie balls with the couscous, mint yoghurt and some extra chopped herbs.

warm butter beans

WITH FRIED BROCCOLI, OLIVE OIL AND HERBS

200 g (7 oz) dried butter beans

1 clove garlic

1 onion

2 sprigs rosemary

150 ml (½ cup) olive oil

salt and freshly ground pepper

juice and zest of 1 organic lemon

1 broccoli head

2 handfuls mixed washed herbs *(sweet cicely, basil, tarragon, garden nasturtium)*

Soak the beans in cold water for 24 hours. The next day, drain the beans and transfer to a pan. Add fresh water to cover the beans by 3–4 cm (1–2 in). Peel the garlic and onion and add to the pan with the beans, together with the rosemary. Bring to the boil. Cook the beans for approx. 35 minutes until tender.

Then transfer two-thirds of the beans to a bowl and season with some salt, pepper and a little olive oil.

Cook the rest of the beans and onion for a further 15 minutes until completely soft. Blend the beans, onion and cooking water with finely grated lemon zest, lemon juice, 50 ml (3 tbsp) olive oil, salt and freshly ground pepper to make a smooth, thick bean puree.

Now add the cooked whole beans to the bean puree and heat everything through. Keep it warm until ready to serve.

Peel the broccoli stalk and cut the broccoli into long florets so that the pieces have both stalk and head. Heat some oil in a pan and fry the broccoli over a high heat for 1–2 minutes so it takes on a nice golden colour but still has plenty of bite. Frying the broccoli a little at a time will make it easier to achieve this. Season with salt and freshly ground pepper, then transfer the broccoli from the pan to a bowl.

Now dish the warm bean mixture into 4 deep plates. Put pieces of fried broccoli on top, drizzle with some olive oil and sprinkle with a good helping of herbs.

steamed mussels

WITH PARSLEY, SPINACH AND MUSSEL BROTH

SERVES 4

1.5 kg (3.5 lb) mussels
1 shallot
1 clove garlic
35 ml (2 tbsp) olive oil
330 ml (1½ cups) beer *(1 can or bottle)*
2 handfuls spinach
1 bunch flat-leaf parsley
30 g (1 oz) butter
salt and freshly ground pepper
1 handful bronze fennel

Rinse and clean the mussels in water, checking that all the mussels are fully closed. If any are open, they must be discarded.

Peel and finely chop the shallot and garlic. Add to a pan along with some olive oil and sauté lightly until the onions are translucent. Add the mussels and stir well. Add the beer and cover. Heat the pan and steam the mussels for 4–5 minutes until they have opened. Don't cook them any longer, as they may become dry or rubbery.

Rinse the parsley and spinach and put in a blender together with cubes of cold butter. Pour the broth from the mussels into the blender and blend to an even light green broth. Season with freshly ground pepper and a little salt if needed.

Transfer the steamed mussels to bowls and pour the warm broth onto them. Sprinkle bronze fennel on top and serve immediately with good bread. An easy, quick, healthy and cheap dinner, and the kids will enjoy eating the mussels with their fingers!

baked potatoes

WITH YOGHURT, PARSLEY OIL, PICKLED RED ONION AND ROAST PORK

SERVES 4

4 large baking potatoes
salt and freshly ground pepper
300 g (10.5 oz) roast pork
1 red onion
35 ml (2 tbsp) apple cider vinegar
200 ml (¾ cup) parsley oil *(see below)*
200 ml (¾ cup) natural yoghurt
40 g (2 oz) freshly grated parmesan

PARSLEY OIL

1 bunch parsley
20 g (1 oz) almonds
200 ml (¾ cup) olive oil
salt and freshly ground pepper

Heat the oven to 180 °C (360 °F). For the parsley oil, rinse the parsley in cold water and drain thoroughly. Blend the parsley leaves with the almonds, olive oil, salt and freshly ground pepper to make a thick oil. Transfer the parsley oil to a bowl and set aside.

Wash the potatoes and place in an ovenproof dish. Sprinkle with a little salt, put in the oven and bake for approx. 1 hour until the potatoes are tender.

While the potatoes are baking, cut the pork into large cubes and fry in a pan until some of the fat has melted and the pork cubes become a little crispy. Take the pork out of the pan and keep it warm.

Peel, halve and finely slice the red onion. Put the onion in a bowl, sprinkle with a little salt and vinegar and mix well, so the onion loses some of its sharpness but keeps a little bite.

Take the potatoes out of the oven. Make a cross cut in the top and squeeze lightly so that they open.

Serve the potatoes with the crispy warm pork pieces, parsley oil, yoghurt and pickled red onion topped with a good helping of freshly grated parmesan. Serve while the potato is still hot so the topping 'melts'.

whole roast chicken

WITH BUTTERMILK, PRESERVED APPLES AND LEMONS, POTATOES,
ONIONS AND GREEN SALAD

SERVES 4–6

1 free-range chicken (1.2–1.5 kg/ 2.5–3.5 lb)

½ litre (2 cups) buttermilk

2 preserved apple cores *(see page 174)*

½ preserved lemon

salt and freshly ground pepper

4 onions

1 kg (2 lb) small potatoes

5 sprigs thyme

50 ml (3 tbsp) olive oil

1 romaine lettuce

Check the chicken for feather stumps and cut out the backbone so that the chicken can lie completely flat. Lightly score the thighs and transfer the chicken to a large bowl. Pour the buttermilk over the chicken. Chop the preserved apple cores and lemon into small pieces and add to the chicken. Season with salt and freshly ground pepper and combine everything together well. Leave the chicken to marinate for 45–60 minutes.

Heat the oven to 170 °C (340 °F). Peel and roughly chop the onions. Put them in the bottom of a large ovenproof dish. Wash and halve the potatoes, then add them to the dish. Season with chopped thyme, salt and freshly ground pepper and mix everything well. Place the chicken on top, pouring the left-over buttermilk marinade over it, and drizzle with olive oil. Season with some extra salt and freshly ground pepper.

Roast the chicken in the oven for 50 minutes. Turn off the heat and let the chicken rest in the closed oven for 10 minutes. Remove the chicken from the oven. It should be beautifully golden with a crispy skin, and the onions and potatoes should be tender.

Cut the lettuce coarsely and rinse in cold water. Let it dry thoroughly.

Carve the chicken and serve with the vegetables and gravy from the dish, the lettuce, suitably dressed, and good bread.

squid fricassee

WITH SOFT CREAMED POTATOES, DRIED CHILLI, SESAME AND PARSLEY

SERVES 4

SQUID FRICASSEE
100 ml (½ cup) olive oil
1 clove garlic
1 tsp dried chilli flakes
600 g (1 lb) fresh squid
    (rinsed weight)
salt and freshly ground pepper
200 ml (¾ cup) white wine
2 tbsp sesame seeds
5 sprigs flat-leaf parsley

CREAMED POTATOES
1 kg (2 lb) potatoes
200 ml (¾ cup) whole milk
100 g (3.5 oz) butter
salt and freshly ground black pepper

For the squid fricassee, heat a deep pan, add the oil, the whole garlic clove and the dried chilli flakes and fry on a low heat for 1 minute so that the oil takes on the flavour of all the ingredients.

Cut the squid (body, tentacles and arms) into very small pieces. Add the pieces to the pan and fry for 5–7 minutes on a low heat so they absorb the flavour of the oil and spices. Season with salt and freshly ground pepper, then add the white wine and let it cook well into the squid to make a dense fricassee. Season to taste with some extra salt and freshly ground pepper if needed. Add the sesame seeds and finely chopped parsley just before serving.

For the soft creamed potatoes, peel the potatoes and add to a pan of unsalted water. Boil for 20–25 minutes until the potatoes are completely tender. Drain the water from the cooked potatoes and let them stand and air-dry in the pot for 2–3 minutes before mashing them.

Warm the milk and cubes of butter in a saucepan until the butter has melted. Mash the warm potatoes, then add the warm milk/butter mixture and stir carefully with a wooden spoon until the milk/butter is fully integrated into the creamed potato. Take care not to stir too much, as the mash can become sticky. The creamed potato should be a little softer in consistency than plain mashed potato. Season to taste with salt and freshly ground pepper and keep the mash warm until serving.

Serve the squid fricassee on top of a good blob of creamed potato and eat straight away.

fried plaice fillet

WITH CAULIFLOWER, TARRAGON, HAZELNUTS AND BROWNED BUTTER

SERVES 4

1 cauliflower
100 ml (½ cup) olive oil
sea salt and freshly ground pepper
10 g (0.5 oz) butter
4 large plaice double fillets
a little rye flour
½ bunch tarragon
30 g (1 oz) hazelnuts
juice and zest of 1 organic lemon

Divide the cauliflower into large florets and fry them in some olive oil over a low heat for 2–3 minutes until browned and slightly tender. Season with salt and freshly ground pepper. Take the cauliflower from the pan and transfer to a bowl, keeping it warm.

Wipe the pan dry, add some oil and the butter and let the butter bubble up. Turn the plaice fillets in some rye flour, then season with salt and freshly ground pepper. Fry the fillets for approx. 1 min on each side until they have a beautiful golden surface but are still juicy in the middle.

Rinse and chop the tarragon. Chop the hazelnuts.

Serve the fillets straight from the pan with the fried cauliflower, chopped tarragon and hazelnuts, finely grated lemon zest, lemon juice and some browned butter from the pan. Enjoy with good bread or rice and a green salad.

ramen

WITH NOODLES, SOFT-BOILED EGG, CHICKEN AND HERBS

SERVES 4

100 g (3.5 oz) dried shitake mushrooms

1 clove garlic

3 lime leaves

1 litre vegetable stock

30 g (1 oz) dried seaweed

juice of 1 lime

4 eggs

200 ml (¾ cup) soy sauce

35 ml (2 tbsp) olive oil

1 chicken breast

salt and freshly ground pepper

100 g (3.5 oz) noodles

2 spring onions

4 radishes

1 fresh red chilli

coriander

2 handfuls pea sprouts

In a saucepan, bring the dried mushrooms, garlic, lime leaves and vegetable stock to the boil. Simmer on a low heat for 5 minutes, then turn off the heat, add the seaweed and lime juice and leave the broth to stand and infuse for 10–15 minutes. Then sieve the broth and return it to the pan.

Bring another pan of water to the boil, add the eggs and cook for 5 minutes. They should be soft-boiled. Transfer the eggs from the pan into cold water so the cooking stops. Then peel the eggs and put them in a bowl with the soy sauce. Leave them to absorb the flavour for 30–45 minutes. Then cut them in halves.

Meanwhile, heat the oil in a frying pan and fry the chicken breast on a medium heat for 5–7 minutes on each side so that it gets a nice roasted crust and is cooked through. Season with salt and freshly ground pepper. Take the chicken breast out of the pan and leave to rest for 5–7 minutes. Slice the chicken when ready to serve.

Pour boiling water over the noodles and let them stand for a couple of minutes. Wash the spring onions and radishes, slice off the tops and roots, then chop finely. Finely slice the chilli.

Now warm the broth and serve in large bowls, adding the slices of chicken, noodles, chilli, sliced radishes and spring onions, and the eggs, with fresh coriander and pea sprouts on top.

Serve the soup while it is still warm and the herbs are still crunchy.

in the
forest

The forests in Denmark offer so much; they change colour with every season. In the spring, when they are light green and delicate, you can gather wild herbs. In the summer they turn a deep, dark green and are filled with bright sunlight and wild berries. In the autumn, brown tones emerge, with the sun shining low through the trees, and the forest is filled with beautiful wild mushrooms and nuts. My family and I spend a lot of time in the forest, foraging for edible things, cooking and enjoying the peace and quiet.

grilled flatbread

WITH MUSHROOMS, BOILED POTATOES, MOZZARELLA, MUSTARD AND PARMESAN

SERVES 4

150 g (5 oz) potatoes
250 g (9 oz) mixed wild mushrooms
 (chanterelles, porcini)
35 ml (2 tbsp) olive oil
salt and freshly ground pepper
5 sprigs fresh thyme
juice and zest of ½ an organic lemon
1 fresh mozzarella
4 flatbreads
2 tbsp mustard
30 g (1 oz) freshly grated parmesan

Boil the potatoes. Meanwhile, clean the mushrooms and cut them into small pieces. Fry in the olive oil for 2–3 minutes until soft and brown. Season with salt and freshly ground pepper, the finely chopped thyme and the lemon juice and zest, finely grated. Remove the mushrooms from the pan.

Slice the boiled potatoes and the mozzarella into thin slices.

Spread mustard on one half of a piece of flatbread, add a thin layer of sliced potato and mozzarella, then the mushrooms, and finally a generous amount of grated parmesan. Season with a little extra salt and freshly ground pepper. Place the other half of the flatbread onto the garnished half and press lightly to make a sandwich.

Toast the flatbread in a sandwich press or on a warm grill pan for 2–3 minutes until it is nicely toasted and warm through. If using a grill, turn the bread halfway through toasting.

Cut the flatbread in half and eat straight away.

fried eggs

WITH CREAMY WILD MUSHROOMS, CORN AND FRIED BREAD

SERVES 4

500 g (18 oz) mixed wild mushrooms
  (porcini, chanterelle, black trumpet)
35 ml (2 tbsp) olive oil
1 corn cob
2 shallots
25 g (1 oz) butter
100 ml (½ cup) whipping cream
juice and zest of 1 organic lemon
salt and pepper
4 slices of day-old bread
4 eggs
½ bunch tarragon

Clean the mushrooms with a brush or small vegetable knife. Rinse carefully with water, if necessary, and allow to dry. Then cut them into small pieces.

Put half the oil in a warm pan, add the mushrooms and fry them for a couple of minutes until they are brown and slightly soft.

Remove the leaves from the corn cob, cut off the kernels and put them in a bowl.

Peel and finely chop the shallots. Then add the shallots and corn kernels to the mushrooms, together with the butter and whipping cream, and allow all the ingredients to 'boil down' into the mushrooms. Season with the finely grated zest and juice of a lemon and a little salt and pepper. Remove the pan from the heat and let the mushroom mixture rest for 1–2 minutes.

Heat another pan, add some of the remaining oil and fry the bread slices until crisp and golden. Remove the bread from the pan, add the rest of the oil and fry the eggs.

Place the bread on a platter or plate and spoon the warm mushrooms onto it. Top with a fried egg and sprinkle with tarragon leaves and freshly ground pepper. Serve for breakfast or lunch or as part of a picnic.

If you can't get wild mushrooms, you can make this dish with button, oyster or beech mushrooms.

grilled porcini mushrooms

WITH DULSE, BUTTERMILK AND EGG YOLK DRESSING

SERVES 4

DRESSING
10 g (⅓) dulse *(sea lettuce or seaweed)*
  (dry weight)
1 egg yolk
50 ml (3 tbsp) buttermilk
35 ml (2 tbsp) apple cider vinegar
salt and freshly ground pepper
500 ml (2 cups) grapeseed oil

MUSHROOMS
500 g (18 oz) porcini mushrooms
wooden skewers
50 ml (3 tbsp) olive oil
salt and freshly ground pepper

For the dressing, soak the dulse in cold water and leave to soften for a couple of hours.

Whisk the egg yolk, buttermilk, vinegar, salt and freshly ground pepper in a blender until evenly mixed and frothy.

Roughly chop the dulse and add to the blender. Continue to blend until it is thoroughly combined with the egg mass. While the blender is still mixing, add drizzles of grapeseed oil until it has all been used and the dressing has reached a creamy consistency.

Pour the dressing into a bowl and season to taste with extra vinegar, salt and freshly ground pepper, if needed.

Clean the mushrooms and cut them into large pieces. Thread the pieces of mushroom onto skewers, drizzle with a little olive oil and season with salt and freshly ground pepper.

Cook the mushroom skewers on a hot grill pan for a couple of minutes on each side until the mushrooms are nicely grilled on the surface.

Eat the mushrooms straight from the skewer and dipped in dressing.

mushroom soup

WITH GRILLED CHICKEN AND CAVOLO NERO

SERVES 4

500 g (18 oz) mixed wild mushrooms
   (porcini, chanterelles, funnel chanterelles,
   black trumpet)
1 shallot
1 clove garlic
35 ml (2 tbsp) olive oil
5 sprigs thyme
sea salt and freshly ground pepper
100 ml (½ cup) dry sherry
1 litre (2 pints) chicken stock
2 chicken breasts
4 branches cavolo nero *(Tuscan/black kale)*
30 g (1 oz) freshly grated parmesan

Clean the mushrooms with a brush or small vegetable knife. Rinse carefully with water, if necessary, and allow to dry. Roughly chop. Peel and finely chop the shallot and garlic.

Pour the olive oil into a large saucepan and sauté the mushrooms, thyme, shallot and garlic until the mushrooms take on a little colour, then season with salt and pepper. Add the sherry to the pan and boil until it has reduced by half. Then add the chicken stock. Let the broth cook for 10–15 minutes so the mushrooms flavour the broth but are still firm. Remove the thyme stalks from the broth and leave it to stand for the flavour to develop while you grill the chicken breasts.

Heat a grill pan. Drizzle the chicken breasts with oil, sprinkle with salt and freshly ground pepper and grill for approx. 5–6 minutes on each side until they are nice and crispy on the surface but still lovely and juicy in the middle. Remove the breasts from the grill pan and let them rest for 5 minutes before cutting into slices.

Rinse the cavolo nero, drain thoroughly and roughly chop.

Divide the slices of chicken breast between 4 soup bowls or deep plates.

Warm the mushroom soup through, season to taste with a little extra salt and pepper if necessary, and ladle the soup into the bowls. Dress the soup with the chopped cavolo nero and grated parmesan, and serve straight away.

Can be served with good bread as a starter, or in a larger portion as a main meal.

pickled chanterelles

WITH SPRUCE, APPLE AND SHALLOTS

1 kg (2 lbs) chanterelle mushrooms

1 litre (2 pints) apple juice *(natural or cloudy, unfiltered and unsweetened)*

1 litre (2 pints) apple cider vinegar

200 g (7 oz) cane sugar

10–15 spruce tips

8 bay leaves

15 whole black peppercorns

2 tbsp sea salt

400 ml (1½ cups) olive oil

4 shallots

2 apples

Clean the chanterelles thoroughly, rinsing if necessary in a large bowl of cold water to ensure that all soil and dirt is removed. Leave to dry on a paper towel.

In a saucepan bring the apple juice, vinegar, sugar, herbs, pepper and salt (including the spruce tips) and olive oil to the boil.

Peel the shallots and cut them in half lengthwise. Remove the core from the apples and cut the rest of the apple into 2 × 2 cm (1 × 1 in) cubes.

When the pickle brine is boiling, add the shallots, apple and chanterelles to the pan and cook on a low heat for 2–3 minutes. Remove the pan from the heat and pour the mixture into a jar, closing it.

Put the jar in the fridge and allow the mushrooms to soak for 4–5 days before eating. An unopened jar of mushrooms will keep for 2–3 months. Once opened, use within 2 weeks.

index

thank you

Anders, lovely to have this book project during these very special times, thank you for your beautiful pictures that make the book something special and the days where we have been able to eat all the wonderful food together with our families and enjoy each other's company, this is important in these times.

Sidsel, for providing all the beautiful things that are in the book, for the loan of your allotment garden and for the many cosy hours with our families.

Julie Kiefer, for giving me the chance to write this book with a foreign publisher, for believing in the project and keeping track of the whole process.

Sigrid Gry Laursen, for the book's beautiful graphic layout, for fighting for all our ideas and wishes and for putting an incredible amount of passion and time into the project.

Samantha Koch, for sparring and feedback, as well as helping me to get the book out into the world.

My mother Anni, who has taught me how important it is to cook good food in your own home, make the effort, gather your family around and spend time eating and enjoying your meals. Thank you, MUTTI!

And my own little family, Viggo, Konrad, Alma, Oscar and Camilla, for taking on the challenges of various food markets on our travels, for tasting the many crazy things we find in nature, and because you have always been curious about food and the meals we enjoy together – it is the best thing to eat and be with you.

© Prestel Verlag, Munich · London · New York, 2021
A member of Penguin Random House Verlagsgruppe GmbH
Neumarkter Strasse 28 · 81673 Munich

Library of Congress Control Number is available;
a CIP catalogue record for this book is available from the British Library.

Editorial direction: Julie Kiefer
Design and layout: Sigrid Gry Laursen
Prop stylist: Sidsel Rudolph
Project management: Sarah Kempff
Translation from Danish: Nina Vickery
Copyediting: Joseph Laredo
Typesetting: Weiß-Freiburg GmbH – Graphik & Buchgestaltung
Production management: Corinna Pickart
Separations: Reproline mediateam
Printing and binding: DZS GRAFIK, d.o.o.
Paper: Magno Natural

Penguin Random House Verlagsgruppe FSC® N001967

Printed in Slovenia

ISBN 978-3-7913-8741-3

www.prestel.com